BIS Publishers
Building Het Sieraad
Postjesweg 1
1057 DT Amsterdam
The Netherlands
T +31 (0)20 515 02 30
bis@bispublishers.com
www.bispublishers.com

ISBN 978 90 6369 414 2

BIS PUBLISHERS

Creative
Chef

By immersing myself in the people and situations I cook for, I reach a maximum effect

I am greatly honoured that you are reading this. It means that you are taking the trouble to get to know more about someone else. I believe the act of placing yourself in someone else's shoes can yield many valuable gifts. In fact, this is the core of what I stand for and what drives me as the Creative Chef. By immersing myself in the people and situations I cook for, I reach a maximum effect! Therefore, I can practice my hobby in such a way that it makes people utterly happy, because someone has taken the trouble to design a unique food experience especially for them.

Why do I love to investigate other people? I'm not sure. I think I bring together a mix of character traits in my role as Creative Chef, with the dominating factor being curiosity. Are you wondering about the other character traits? All right, here goes: I'm lazy and diligent at the same time and I love people. Moreover, I grew up in the kitchens of my mother and my grandparents. My father is a real gourmand, and my first holiday memory is of an old Frenchman devouring a plate of oysters while my father enjoyed a quail with its little head still attached.

All my memories are focused on food experiences, my holidays are centred around food and I feel that preparing food is the best meditation there is to quiet my head. After all, my head is also full with other things! My wife and children play the lead roles (including what I will be cooking for them) and it continues with music and art. Making music is, after cooking, the coolest thing to do. I play the drums in various bands and collect vinyl records. I also enjoy recording music and listening to it over and over again. And then art... Yeah, man, that's my greatest source of inspiration. People and their stories about what art is, beautiful pictures, design, graphics, comics, fashion... You name it, I take it all in. And what do I do with it?

Practice entrepreneurship, create opportunities and go for what I believe in. That is also the basis from which this book has emerged. A book that was written with the belief that eating with friends can be even more fun if you pay attention to the small details and consider your guests. This ensures that you will not just be cooking for yourself, to demonstrate your skills, but instead you'll be cooking to suit the character of your guests. This is what the Creative Chef stands for. "Do you do everything by yourself then?" I hear you think. No, Creative Chef also stands for co-creation and collaboration. Fun projects improve when you collaborate with the right people. I love working with architects, photographers, stylists, consultants, furniture makers, designers, entrepreneurs and anyone who believes in co-creation. So, if you ever feel you have a good idea...

Wishing you lots of inspiration!

Jasper Udink ten Cate

COLOPHON

Author: Jasper Udink ten Cate
Editor: Luc Janssens and Bis Publishers
Art direction, design and illustrations: subsoda
Photography and Direction: Rogier Boogaard
Photography; Bas van Hattum, Elise Yuksl, Marjon Hogervorst,
Warni van Mierlo, Timo Venhuis, Irina Raiu, Floris Heuer,
Wouter de Winter, Bas Berkhout and subsoda
Other contributions; USE Architects, Reinder Eekhof,
Carel Huydecoper, Jeannot Nijpjes, Ronald van der Heide,
Reinier Suurenbroek, Varkensroosteren.nl

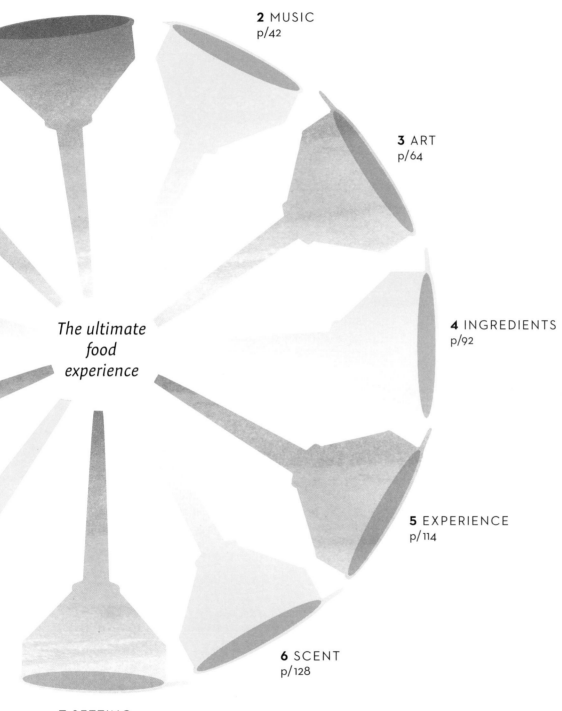

Presentation is an important aspect of the ultimate food experience. You can impress people with your skills in arranging the plates, but you could also play with the plate you serve the food on! Or you might just enjoy presenting the food entirely differently for once.

Presentation examples
to let go of the 'serving food on plates' rule!

Baking paper:
spread it out on your dinner table and throw all your food on it.

Field hockey stick:
serve some meatballs on it

Vinyl record:
put on a pick up and serve some sushi on it

Present:
serve your food like a present

Cactus:
put some snacks on the needles

Paint tray:
french fries with ketchup

Fishing rod:
with a fried fish

Table tennis bat:
with a scoop of ice cream

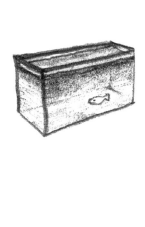

Use your old aquarium to serve some good bouillabaisse fish soup!

Knapsack:

serve your bread in it

Bonsai tree:

put some snacks on it

Ironing board:

serve with grilled cheese sandwich and iron

Saw:

serve some Battenbergs on it with a spoon and toast

Toy truck:

to persuade your children to eat vegetables

A real sword

with pieces of meat from the BBQ

Door:

use as a massive serving plate for massive portions

A hollow book

with a dish in it and how to make it on the other page

Newspaper:

with fish and chips, on a "good news" page

HAPPY HOUR CACTUS

Inspiringly delicious! *Please note: do not use just any cactus; ask the*
cactus vendor for one without poisonous spines.
Also use for Mexican mini-wraps, sweets or just strawberries!

TOSTIS

Super fun to serve from behind an ironing board. Delicious
grilled cheese sandwich with white bread and cheese.

QUANTUMMMM...

Okay, let me challenge you as a reader. No, don't skip to the next page just yet and give it a try. How do your present a dish or dinner with a difficult theme? For instance, imagine you are asked to prepare a dinner for various whizzes around the theme 'quantum mechanics'.
Man. That's no small feat. I know something about Einstein and the fact that he did something with 'quantum mechanics', but I can tell you: I know nothing about it!

So, let's think about this! What would you do? In the meantime, I'll start brainstorming on the page to the right.

QWANTUM FOOD EXPERIENCE...
MMMM... I THINK ABOUT
'MOLECULES'... SCIENTIFIC
ATLAS... STAR WARS AND
MR. SPOCK AND THE ENTERPRISE...
- INTERGALACTIC OF
THE BEASTIE BOYS,
GREAT MUSIC! - LUKE... I AM
YOUR FATHER - COMICS... THE
CHALLENGER. GALAXY. MILK' WAY...
<?!*^%!#&*(> YEAHHH

I GOT IT! ...

A dinner party between the stars

Okay, this is the final result. A super snack board with an intergalactic and highly entertaining character. I named all bites after space phenomena and served them on a map of the Milky Way. Put on spacy music and introduce yourself to the guests coming in as Dr. Cook, *the best cook from outer space.*

The you tell them a story of intergalactic proportions with exploding aliens in the form of edible insects, flying octopuses, freeze-dried vegetable domes, snack molecules and of course a bit of paracress, but then on a map of the Milky Way!

OCTOPUSSY CHALLENGERS

> Small octopus
> Garlic olive oil
> Lemon

Heat the oil in a pan. Fry the octopuses in the hot oil. Also add a clove of garlic and deglaze with lemon juice. Fry the whole mix very briefly! Serve it on the star map as formidable opponents of the space hoppers.

Use the next page to suggest some cosmic explosions. Stick them to foam board and cut them out with the use of a utility knife.

SNACK MOLECULES

> Skewers
> Appetizers such as cheese, olives, sausage and gherkins.

MOTHERSHIP GALACTICA

SPACE HOPPER

> Freeze-dried grasshoppers
> Carrot juice
> Olive oil

Heat some olive oil in the frying pan. Remove the wings of the grasshoppers. Let the oil get very hot and briefly fry the grasshoppers. Add some carrot juice and let it evaporate very quickly. Now a beautiful sweet carrot glazing should have formed around the grasshoppers, which makes them extremely tasty. You can use these as galactite spacehopper spaceships, which engage in battle with:

SPACE LIQUIDS

> Tomato juice
> Prosecco
> Soy milk
> Juice of mostarda di cremona
> Soy sauce
> Cucumber

Mix all the ingredients in the food processor until they are fine and fill small glasses - or in my case, spacey balls with a cap!
Also consider using test tubes or toy water guns that you can fill with the space liquid.

SALMON SPACE CENTRES

> Salmon and tuna (raw)
> Yuzu
> Edible silver paint
> Trout caviar
> Oyster leaf

Create a few space centres with sashimi of salmon and tuna on the star map. Preferably with sustainable hamachi tuna and of course wild salmon. Soak the fish very briefly in some yuzu. Make neat little piles/structures with the fish and finish them with sunscreens from oyster leaf and sun-repellent coating of pieces of trout and a spray bottle with edible silver paint.

PLANETS

Spheres/bowls from Ikea
Vegetable crisps/nuts, and anything else you would like to serve with the intergalactic snack platter!

Dianthus flowers

Anise flowers

Licorice plant

Chive flowers

Pond pump

Cosmea flowers

Edible pond

Picking the fresh ingredients is quite an experience, but how can you take that experience - the place your flavours come from - and incorporate it into your dish? Right, by being creative. Present a mini-version of a pond and fancy yourself in a beautiful natural landscape, in which you and your guests can fish out your food directly from the pond.

POND

> **A large basin that can serve as the pond**
> **A small pond pump**
> **Reed**
> **Milk bottles**

Prepare the basin in a nice place near a power socket. Place the pond pomp and hide the plug a bit between two milk bottles, which you fill with water some reed stems. Please note: you cannot eat those!

BROTH

> **Seaweed**
> **White wine**
> **Leek**
> **Mussel juice**

Boil equal parts water and white wine in a large pan of for instance ten liters and add seaweed and leek. Sieve the broth and add the mussels. Bring to a boil until they open up and slightly let it cool off. Sieve once again (otherwise your pond pump will get clogged) and add the mussels to the large basin that will serve as your pond.

SERVE

> **Broth**
> **Bouquet of edible flowers (or vegetables such as celery and leek)**

Add the cooled off broth to the basin with the mussels and finish off the edible flowers.
TIP: Fish out the mussels fresh from the pond!

ACCORDING TO THE RULES

OK, and how do you present dishes on plates? The Creative Chef has some ideas for that, too. Round plates, straight lines, crooked lines, building little towers, some colours, square plates...
The possibilities are endless! I hereby offer you a number of fixed forms that I use whenever I am at a loss. Let yourself be inspired by these three fixed presentations and apply them to your own plates!

ROUNDABOUT

Cucumber, beans, lemon cucumber, fennel, tomato, Indian cress, and a clear vegetable broth with lavender.

SQUARE

Beetroot, flowers, onions, chard and ham.

ZEN

Fennel, fennel flowers, sardines
in lemon, squid ink.

A forest on your plate

SLOW-COOKED BOAR POT ROAST WITH FRIED MUSHROOMS AND VEGETABLE CRISPS

The most beautiful dish to land on this plate is of course something with freshly picked mushrooms, roasted chestnuts, roasted beechnuts and fern tops served with ragout of wild boar. However, the average home cook might not be so likely to go to all that trouble, so I'll stick to ingredients that are fairly easy to get from the better specialists.

SLOW-COOKED CARBONNADE FLAMANDE

> 500 grams wild boar cheeks without membrane
> 2 onions
> 1/2 bottle of red wine
> 1/2 litre game broth
> 2 juniper berries
> 1 bay leaf
> 100 grams butter

Fry the cheeks in the frying pan. Transfer them to a saucepan and add the wine and the broth. Furthermore, add large chunks of onion and in the meantime put on a record of, for instance, Jimi Hendrix. Let the dish cook very softly over the span of four hours. Remove the meat from the pan and sieve the liquid. Boil down the liquid to 1/3 and add a cold knob of butter until the sauce binds.

MUSHROOMS

> 250 grams of wild mushrooms
Clean the mushrooms and fry them with a pinch of salt in the frying pan.

SERVE

> Plate with a bouquet on it
> Assortment of vegetable crisps from the store
Place the meat on the plate with a bouquet on it. Generously pour the sauce over it, including the fried mushrooms.
Crumble the vegetable crisps and sprinkle over the dish. Serve with a spoon. The meat is so tender, it can be spooned!

SERVING TIP

> Crowded House LP Woodface
> Creative Chef perfume No. 02
  (Chapter 6 Scent)
> Game dishes such as jugged hare or vegetarian dishes on the basis of mushrooms

The phenomenon of 'arranging plates' was invented in the Russian Court

DINING WITH THE TSARS

I've always been fascinated by the stories of the Russian Tsars. I always used to imagine how those grand dinners must have been at that time. And you know what: that was quite something. The Russians have invented dining as we now know it. Grand tables, splendid china and of course Russian dishes.

Because the Russian elite made such a big deal out of their dinners, the platters, plates and chalices became increasingly bigger. They started to take up more and more space on the table, so dinners in old Russia became a logistical nightmare. The chefs started arranging the dishes on the plates in an appealing manner and serving them per person. So, no more large platters and showpieces, but small, single-serve dishes on a pretty plate.

"Where is the Creative Chef going with this story?" I hear you think. Well, it's great to tell your guests a story about Tsars and their eating habits when you are yourself doing your best to create a 'Tsar-worthy ' dish... Don't you agree?

RUSSIAN ALLURE

Let your guests dig in with a dish of Russian allure: blini with smoked salmon, caviar and crème fraîche. In addition, you offer all sorts of ingredients to arrange the plate extra beautifully, just like in olden days, in which the beauty of the plate was more important than the actual taste of the dish.

> Porcelain plates were also referred to as white gold?
> Porcelain owes its name to Marco Polo. Marco brought it back from China, and described it as: 'smooth, hard and transparent like the house of the porcella' (type of sea snail)!
> At the thrift shop you will often find very ugly and very beautiful examples that will perfectly match your themed dinner. And it hardly costs anything!
> Your food will taste much better from a pretty and unique plate! Imagine having your favourite dish served to you on a 2000-year old plate!
> Tip: break a plate by throwing it and serve Greek finger food on the shards, get it?

1

Start with cold dishes so that you can ease into practicing and getting the techniques down.

2

Try using paintings from Mondriaan as a reference point!

3

Think in lines. Even if you arrange your plate in a circle or around a centre, lines can make the dish more appealing.

10

Check the internet for tricks, such as making a quenelle.

Tips and Tricks to style your plate that you can share with your guests

4

Work vertically. Also do this with lines.

9

Think in terms of colours, use colours that contrast with each other (yellow and purple), or rather opt for something peaceful (only green).

5

Opt for either organic lines (so more curving) or really straight ones.

8

Try to involve the environment. In other words: how can the plate contribute to the dish? What colour is the plate? Does the plate have patterns that you can use for the arrangement?

7

Go crazy and serve the dish on something other than a plate!

6

Purchase a Parisienne scoop or skewers to form your vegetables into neat balls.

The result:

Beautiful plates with a first course your guests personally plated.

At the end of the evening

you announce the winner who made the best plate.

TSAR DINNER RECIPE

The recipe around which the guests were invited to arrange their plates was based on a classic and highly delicious recipe from Russia.

COCKTAIL WITH A KICK

This cocktail is a mix between the famous Russian beetroot soup Borscht and a Bloody Mary. The tastes represent the feeling I get when I think of Russia. Powerful, pure tastes and it takes some perseverance, but afterwards you will be fully refreshed and feel nice and warm!

> 1 shot of vodka
> 1 shot of beetroot juice
> 1 shot of freshly squeezed apple juice
> 2 drops of edible pine tree water (see chapter on Scent)
> 1 pinch of porcini powder
> ice cubes
> 1 teaspoon of yoghurt
> 1 teaspoon of honey

Place all the ingredients, except the honey and the yoghurt, in the mixer and blend until you have a fine mixture. Serve in a glass and drink in one go, followed by one spoon of honey and one spoon of yoghurt.

SERVING TIP

> *Hide the glass in a Matryoshka doll*
> *Give the guests a Russian dictionary so they can get in a Russian mood.*
> *Call out "Nostrovia!" upon drinking*

BLINI WITH SOUR CREAM AND SALMON

> 250 ml milk
> 8 grams of instant yeast
> 200 grams of buckwheat flour
> 1 tsp. sugar
> pinch of salt
> 60 grams of butter
> 2 egg yolks
> 2 stiffly whipped egg whites

Heat the milk until lukewarm and add the yeast, and in phases the flour, the butter, the salt and some sugar. Whisk well, store separately in the fridge and leave it to rise for 2 hours. Then fold in the egg yolks and the stiffly whipped egg whites. Carefully fry the small blinis in a frying pan with the use of a frying ring. Do not cook more than four at a time. Keep the blinis warm in an oven. Serve with sour cream and smoked salmon.

SERVING TIP

You can best eat these with heavy Russian literature. So go ahead and pour yourself some vodka, sink back into a lazy armchair, grab a book of Tolstoy or Dostoyevsky and keep eating these blinis. Apparently, Russians never stop eating them either. Should this sound too heavy, then serve them up for a Russian Film night.

Some suggestions:
From Russia with Love, Pantzerkruizer Potemkin, or listen to the entire play of 'Peter and the Wolf' by Sergei Prokofiev on your stereo system.

Let's make food, not war

CAMOUFLAGE SALAD

SALAD

> Old army helmet
> Shiso leaf
> Romaine lettuce
> Radicchio
> Fresh dill
> Fresh tarragon
> Four boiled eggs

Add all ingredients to a large bowl and chop the dill and tarragon really fine. Be careful not to hold back with the herbs!
Pour all the salad into the helmet and place it on the table. Serve with the dressing.

DRESSING

> 1 tablespoon algae powder
> 1 apple
> 2 teaspoons vinegar
> 1 tablespoon mustard
> Grape seed oil

Process the apple with the juicer and collect the juice.
Mix two tablespoons with the algae, the vinegar and the mustard.
Slowly pour the grape seed oil into the mix until the dressing reaches yoghurt thickness!

SERVING TIP

Music: Born to be Wild by Steppenwolf
Scent: Perfume No. 3 (you can find the recipe in chapter 6)
Perhaps do something creative with canteens, ration cans and bullet casings?

THE TASTE OF MUSIC

Music is a wondrous art form. It subconsciously influences your mood and experience of a film, for instance. And, how cool: it gives you goose bumps! I am utterly convinced that music also influences your food experience.

A fried scallop with cucumber gravy doesn't go together as well with Heavy Metal as it does with the soundtrack from The Little Mermaid... Although...

GAZPACHO

with Spanish flamenco music

> 1 kg of tomatoes
> 1 cucumber
> 1 shallot
> 2 cloves of garlic
> 2 slices of white bread with the crusts removed
> Paracress
> Half a red pepper without seeds
> White wine vinegar
> Sugar
> Oil
> Salt
> Headphones and MP3 player
> Flamenco music

Fill the blender with the tomatoes, shallot, garlic and cucumber. Blend into a fine mix and sieve through a fine strainer. Place back in the blender and, while it's running, add the bread, vinegar and some salt. Taste the mixture and add a bit more of the aforementioned ingredients to taste. Run the blender for a bit more and then add a bit of oil for the taste and to bind the mixture. Switch on the music and experience!

FRIED GRASSHOPPER

with Paganini

> **Freeze-dried grasshoppers**
> **Rice flour**
> **Ice-cold sparkling mineral water**
> **Deep-frying pan with arachis oil at 180 degrees**
> **Headphones and MP3 player**
> **Flight of the Bumble Bee by Paganini**

Make a runny porridge of water and rice flour (lumps are allowed). Dip the grasshopper in the mixture and fry. Serve with a dip sauce or, even better, with honey. Put on a rendition of Flight of the Bumble Bee by Paganini and experience!

CHOCOLATE BONBON

with Alle Menschen werden Brüder

> 1 dl whipped cream
> 200 grams dark chocolate
> 1 tsp. (espresso) instant coffee
> 1 tbsp. Grand Marnier
> 1 tsp. powdered sugar
> Paper bonbon moulds
> Headphones and MP3 player
> Beethoven's 9th Symphony

Heat up 1 bag of shelled walnuts (garnish) in a saucepan with cream. Take off the fire and break the chocolate in pieces above the pan. Let the pieces melt while stirring. Sir into the mix: instant coffee, Grand Marnier and powdered sugar. Place the chocolate mixture in a cool spot and let it set. Then transfer to a pastry bag with a star-shaped spout. Squeeze into the paper moulds and garnish with half a walnut. Let the bonbons dry in a cool place. Put on a performance of Alle Menschen werden Brüder from Beethoven's 9th Symphony! An easy and heavenly chocolate bonbon; close your eyes and experience this music while you slowly chew the bonbon!

Headphones with your dishes provide extra enjoyment.

Turn your food into a taste concert.

Creative
Chef

Chocolate sounds like
music to your ears

How do I make a vinyl record from chocolate?

One that can actually play music!

Use dark chocolate with a low percentage of cocoa butter.

Supplies; A record, preferably from bakelite, as those grooves are nice and deep.

Create a mould from the record with the use of silicones.

Play the record in a space with a low temperature! It will really work!

Pour the chocolate into the mould.

Creative Chef's
SOUL BURGER

BURGER
> 600 grams of blade steak with fat
> 60 grams of pistachio nuts
> 1 tbsp. cajun spices
> 5 grams of salt

Cut the meat into cubes. Put them through the meat processor or grind into a fine mixture in the food processor. Add the spices and the pistachios and make four burger patties from it. Place them on a plate on the speaker of your sound system and let the burgers marinate in sultry soul music.

SAUCE
> 1 onion
> 1 celery stalk
> 1 clove of garlic
> 1 tsp. maple syrup
> 1 tbsp. apple cider vinegar
> 1 tbsp. tomato paste
> 1 tbsp. worcestershire sauce

Chop an onion into fine pieces to the rhythm of the marinade music. On the chorus of the marinade music, hit the frying pan with a stalk of celery and place it on the fire. Crush the garlic on the 1st count of the second verse and add some oil in the pan. The music can use some percussion, so we'll imitate some shakers by adding onions and garlic to the hot frying pan. Then chop the celery stalks in rhythmic cubes and regularly hit the bottles of apple cider vinegar, maple syrup and worcestershire sauce with your knife. Then add this with the tomato paste and tap the pan with a spoon. In the meantime, stir everything well and let the sauce boil down to a syrupy and funky sauce.

FINISH

> **Leaves of lettuce**
> **Slices tomato**
> **Cheddar**
> **Carrot**
> **Hamburger buns**
> **Headphones and MP3 player**

Cut the bun and add the lettuce. Chop the tomato in rhythmic slices and, in the meantime, place the frying pan on the fire with some sizzling oil. Place the burgers in the pan and fry them medium rare. They should still be red on the inside! This takes about eight minutes. Remove them from the pan and place the slices of cheese on top. Let them melt and place the patties on the buns. Add the sauce to the burger and finish with the top bun. Place a skewer through the burger and place headphones on it, naturally with soul music.

SIDE DISH: FRIES

Buy a second-hand copy of the record that you enjoy listening to during your soul dinner. Place the record on a warm pan until it starts getting soft and melting. This creates a beautiful bowl. Add a napkin and throw in the fries. The hamburgers can be served on the record cover.

What do I serve my fries in? In a vinyl record!

DIG IN Y'ALL

CHOCOLATE MIXTAPE

Back in the day, I used to make mixtapes for others!
A cassette tape with various hit songs that I wanted
to share with the other person to let them know I
liked them, or even to let it shine through that I was
in love!

You can do the same with food! Imagine you are in love with a girl. Girls
love chocolate!

Use silicones or clay to make a mould around a cassette tape. Melt the
chocolate and pour into the mould. Write the all the songs you want that
person to listen to while eating the chocolate on the track list. Then share
that track list with her through internet.

If that doesn't make her yours, I don't know what will!

ASIDE

Peter ... Moraine ...
Extreme - (Every Thing)
Bryan Adams ...

GROOVY TOMATO SOUP

Food and kitchenware that make noise in order to funk up your cooking routine! You are truly the ultimate boss if you have a looping station at home. In that case, you can use these ingredients and sounds to record a drum composition.

Set your egg timer! This is your metronome! *OK, count down four beats and press on the 1 beat on your looping station* Crush your **garlic**

BAM Crush the garlic on the 1st and 3rd beats *Crack*

Crush a 100 grams of **almonds** with a knife. Do this on the second beat and place in a bowl. You have now created the basic rhythm;

BAM....Crack.....BAM.....Crack

That can do with some percussion! **Chopping an onion**

chuck chuck

Chop the onion in half and dice into small pieces on the 1st and 2nd and the 3rd and the 4th

chuck chuck chuck chuck BAM... Crack.. BAM...Crack

Ok, let's bring some life into the rhythm now... **Pan with butter**

Tssssssssshhhhhhht

Add the onion and the garlic in the pan and let it fry

Chop the carrot into rough chunks on the *2nd padam pom* and the 4th *padam pom*

Carrot chop

Tssssssssshhhhhhht Tssssssssshhhhhhht Tsssssss - shhhhhht Tssssssssshhhhhhht chop chop chuck chuck

Ok, time to do some rapping and singing and whistling using the wine bottle which is getting emptier by the second! Open a bag of crisps to nibble and the packaging of that bag sounds wicked! PLEASE NOTE you have 10 minutes for this while the soup simmers.

toinggg Tsssssshhhht Tsssssshhhht sssssssss Tshhhhhhht Tssssssshhhht chop chop chuck chuck chuck

Crisps crisp

Pots and pans Klunk Klunk Kitchen worktop Clap Plates and cutlery Ping Ping vreeeeeeeeew Glass Ting ting ting vreeeeeeeeew Tssssssssshhhhhht Tssssssssshhhhhht Tssssssssshhhhhht Tssssssssshhhhhht

Open **a can of tomatoes** and ensure you don't entirely cut off the lid with the can opener. Add the tomato to the pan and pull the lid on the 2nd, so it starts to tremble nicely.

toinggg

Grab the blender

zuuuffff

Add some cream to the soup and blend it finely on the 1st and 2nd and 3rd and *zuuuffff* 4th. Finish with salt and pepper and serve with some crushed almonds in it!

zuuuffff zuuuffff toinggg sssssssssshhhhhhht sssssssss - shhhhhht sssssssssshhhhhhht sssssssssshhhhhhht chop chop chuck chuck chuck BAM.... Crack..... BAM..... Crack

PLAYLISTS

I have asked my favourite artists at DOX Records to make a list of their favourite songs for during dinner, making food, or related to food. You can listen to the lists on my website by scanning with your phone.

WOUTER HAMEL

FELIX SCHLARMANN

CIRQUE VALENTIN

MY FAVOURITE TEN OLDIES ABOUT FOOD

> *Come-On-A-My House - Della Reese (Della Della Cha Cha Cha)*
> *Hold Tight (Want Some Seafood, Mama) - Fats Waller (My Story)*
> *Home Cookin` - Lambert, Hendricks & Ross (The Hottest New Group in Jazz)*
> *Put More Food on the Fire - Eartha Kitt*
> *Everybody Eats When They Come to My House - Cab Calloway & His Orchestra (Are You Hep to the Jive?)*
> *I Can Cook Too - Nancy Walker (Wonderful Town)*
> *Charleston Alley - Lambert, Hendricks & Ross (The Hottest New Group in Jazz)*
> *Sing For Your Supper - Mel Tormé (The Velvet Fog)*
> *That Chick's Too Young to Fry - Louis Jordan (Easy Does It)*
> *Dinner For One Please, James - Eartha Kitt (The Essential Eartha Kitt)*

KOFFIE

TOP 10 DINER A DEUX

> *Lisliel - David Binney*
> *Northern Light - Seamus Blake*
> *Evening Song - Jakob Bro*
> *Follow - Celine Cairo*
> *Homecoming - Jasper Blom Quartet*
> *Polly Come Home - Robert Plant*
> *Choosing Sides - ERIMAJ*
> *It's Been So Long - Avishai Cohen*
> *Everything Must Change - Nils Landgren*
> *Both Sides Now - Joni Mitchell*

SNACK HOUSE

> *Club Tropicana - Wham*
> *Together Again - Janet Jackson*
> *Move Your Feet - Junior Senior*
> *Don't Phunk With My Heart - Black Eyed Peas*
> *Toxic - Britney Spears*
> *Club Tido (Radio Edit) - Cirque Valentin*
> *Mambo No. 5 - Lou Bega (A Little Bit Of..)*
> *Call Me Maybe - Carly Rae Jepsen*
> *Temperature - Sean Paul*
> *Lay Up Under Me - Beyonce*
> *Will 2K - Will Smith*

SOUL FOOD

> *Gentleman - Fela*
> *Born under punches - Talking Heads*
> *Melody day - Caribou*
> *The Hurricane - Bob Dylan*
> *Heaven - Ebo Taylor*
> *Complex - Photek*
> *Bukom Mashie - Oscar Sulley & The Uhuru Dance Band*
> *Yegelle tezeta - Mulatu Astatke*
> *Um So - Pedro Santos*
> *Sympathy for the Devil - Rolling Stones*

CHARLENE

TOP 10 SONGS DURING COOKING

> Burial - Miike Snow
> Kangaroo Court - Capital Cities
> Ritual Union - Little Dragon
> What about us - Flume & Chet Faker
> Losing you - Solange
> Rescue Song RAC Remix - Mr Little Jeans
> Magic - Coldplay
> Midnight City - M83
> You stood me up - Benji Hughes
> Song for no one - Miike Snow

ROOS JONKER

BREAKFAST SONGS

> Radio - KLARA
> Say it over and over again - John Coltrane
> My one and only love - Johnny Hartman & John Coltrane
> Long, Long Day - Paul Simon
> Anders - Herman van Veen
> One Man's Dream - Cannonball Adderley
> You won't be satisfied until you break my heart - Doris Day
> She's out of my life (demo version this is it) - Michael Jackson
> Through the morning through the night - Allison Krauss & Robert Plant
> Honeysuckle Rose - Ella Fitzgerald & Count Basie

DJ MAESTRO

A DINNER TO KILL FOR...

> Music to be murdered by - Jeff Alexander, Alfred Hitchcock
> Bags Groove - Bobby Jaspar
> Danse - Andre Odeir
> Parlez moi de velours - The diamond Five
> Table Cloth Stomp - Bobby Scott
> Theme de liz - Andre Goraguer orchestra
> Final au Jardin d'acclimation - Barney Wilen

GIOVANCA

DINNER ON THE ROAD

> When you were mine - Prince
> Rosa Parks - Outkast
> Driver's seat - Sniff 'n the Tears
> It's a family affair - Sly & The Family Stone
> We need a resolution - Aaliyah
> Fantasy - Earth Wind & Fire
> I love you - Mary J. Blige
> Me gustas tu - Manu Chau
> Got to give it up - Marvin Gaye
> Sally - Bilal

SOUL FOOD

I love soul music. And apart from the music sounds,
I always associate soul music with large afro hairdos.
So when I have to serve food at a music festival, why
not serve it in the form of a huge afro!

If you are good at drawing - like Ruben Ramos, who made the image on
this page - you can easily make the basis yourself, but you can also use
a projector to trace well-known artists on a canvas cloth. For instance,
I'm thinking of:

Jimi Hendrix

Aretha Franklin

Michael Jackson

Art Blakey

Run DMC

DISHES IN THE FORM OF AN AFRO

When I serve an afro, I usually make a Hairy Salad.
Bowls made from palm leaf with a salad of colourful vegetables and edible
flowers. Of course, there are many more options that you could serve. For
instance, what do you think of the following 'Hairy Snacks'?

Doughnuts
Cupcakes
Seafood such as mussels and crabs
Spaghetti
Biscuits
Sweets
Mini-hamburgers

MARKETING STRATEGY

Treat your dinner like a famous band. That works really well and opens up a range of possibilities for involving your guests in the brand of your dinner beforehand! Here are some tips with content you can send them.

The Cooks

On a world tour to bring you some Hot Hits, such as:

THEIR SENSATIONAL NO. 1 SINGLE:
1. Pulled Pork Tonight
(with red hot chili pepper sauce)

THEIR SMOOTH AND JUICY:
2. The Beef Song
(with groovy gravy and flower power)

THEIR CLASSIC EVERGREEN:
3. Like a Smashed Potato
(with some creamy chops and black eyed peas)

FRESH FROM THEIR STUDIO:
4. Do the Wrap & Roll
(with some spicy notes)

THEIR LATEST SUCCESS:
5. Give Me a Piece of Your Steak Now
(with some fried green onions)

AND, OF COURSE, THEIR WORLDWIDE SUPER HIT:
6. Cook & Stove
(with some chickens and wild cherrywood)

Fashion your invitation from a record sleeve.

As soon as your dinner is nearly fully booked, set up a competition. The winner gets the last two seats for a delicious concert by The Cooks.

Let your guests show their tickets upon arrival.

Have some t-shirts printed. Naturally, a real band has its merchandising in order.

A Famous Dinner

Serve a remix instead of drinks.

Champagne with a bit of ginger beer.

A can of festival beer with lemonade.

Red wine with cubes of ice.

Place a crush barrier near the kitchen and hang up some old disco lights.

Upon opening the buffet, hand out backstage passes or armbands.

A PAINTING YOU
COULD JUST EAT UP

Art plays an important role in our lives, often without us even realising it. Everywhere around us we see design: products in the supermarket, postcards, menus, etc. How do you think our visual language has evolved into what it is today?

The painter has the canvas, the actor the theatre, the musician the stage and... exactly, **the chef has the plate!**

At the foundation of a creative expression there is always a creative person. For instance, think of architects, furniture makers, clothing designers and graphic designers. But what about chefs?

Edible paintings! That's what
I enjoy making most. The
experience of the making is a
true joy, and the best thing is:
you in turn create an experience
for your guests!

SERVING SUGGESTION

> *If you make a painting for ten people, you only need to serve one plate!*
> *For the extra wow factor, place a nice frame around the artwork.*
> *Works nicely for a children's party.*
> *Let your guests have at it with a fork: the stain pattern that emerges will
> certainly yield a beautiful end result!*

THE PAINTER

Put on your favourite music and let the canvas have it!
I can greatly recommend the following thoughts:

> *Woohoooo, let's get that paint rolling!*
> *OK, moving on to a smoother tune (a little Frank Zappa does the trick for us).*
> *What would happen if I shoot the paint onto the canvas with a Super Soaker?*
> *It was such a good idea to do this!*

Avoid thoughts such as:

> *Should this not resemble something?*
> *I'm not really all that creative.*
> *Will this still taste all right?*
> *I'm not actually able to make a painting.*
> *Oh, man, there's so much I still need to get done today!*

THE EXHIBITION

Serve the painting to your guests and, by all means, let them share it on social media. Your artwork deserves an exhibition before it gets eaten!

How do you create a painting that you could just eat up?

THE INGREDIENTS

The other ingredients to use in your painting can be chosen according to your own vision and taste. Colourful ingredients work well, for instance vegetable crisps, edible flowers, bread, cake, ginger snaps, nori sheets, and spaghetti for making lines. Of course, there is sooooo much more to come up with.

THE PAINTING

Scrape off the leftovers from the canvas after dinner and let the canvas dry for day.
Then impregnate it with hairspray, for instance.
TIP: don't attempt to do this with paintings that were used to eat meat or fish from! Trust me, you do not want to do that...

SHOPPING LIST

> *Linen cloths (art supply store)*
> *Palette knife*
> *Brushes*
> *Artist's palette*
> *Canvas*
> *Fixer*

THE PAINT

You have so many options for this! Determine for yourself what kind of dish you wish to make, savoury or sweet. If you opt for sweet, you can make your base paint out of white chocolate mousse, for example. Should you opt for savoury, then the base paint can be made out of yoghurt or agar. Use the colour chart as a guide for your shopping trip.

GET INSPIRED

Go to a bookstore and buy an art book to get inspired by abstract artists. Or take sneaky pictures of paintings you like.

A Delicious— and Random Composition

A Delicious and Random Composition
Creative Chef and 117 unknown dinner
guests, 2014
Materials: edible colourants, marzipan,
whipped cream, fruit and biscuits on linen

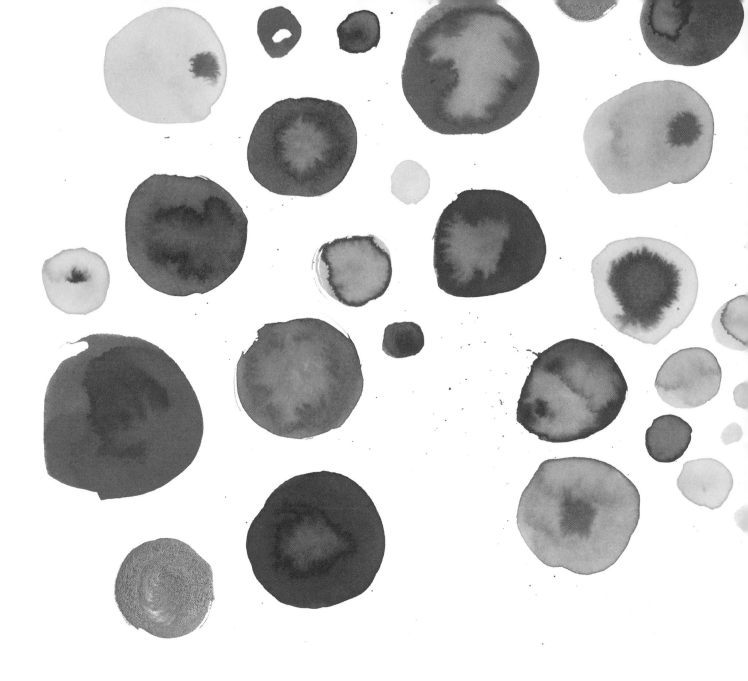

THE COLOUR CHART

TYPES OF PAINT

~ oil-based
Mix 1 egg yolk with colourant and slowly stir in some oil* with a whisk until the mixture binds.

*Use sunflower or grapeseed oil. Olive oil usually makes this paint unpleasantly bitter.

~ a basis of white, paint-like substances...
...such as yoghurt, crème fraîche, whipped cream, white chocolate mousse, mayonnaise, Béarnaise sauce or garlic sauce. Mix these substances with a colourant of your choice.

~ a basis of fruit or vegetable juice and agar
Blend these gelatinous substances into a fine mixture with the food processor, so that you create a clear and sometimes transparent type of paint.

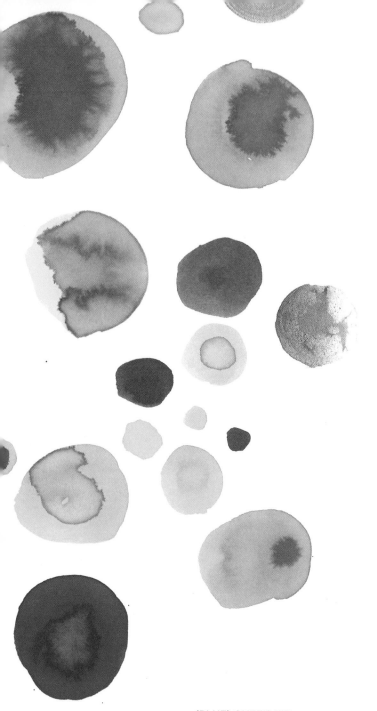

COLOURANTS

Colourants from the patisserie
These are fantastic to use! They have really intense colours that mix well with various basic materials. You can also get patisserie colourants in a spray can, ideal if you like graffiti.

(BLUE) CHEF'S TIP

Boil red cabbage leaves in a pan with water that has some baking soda added to it. The cooking liquid will turn blue. This liquid can be boiled down to arrive at a reasonable blue colour. Other than that, blue is quite difficult to achieve. I often use blue colourant that is commonly used for marzipan and other blue sweets. Of course, this is not a natural product, so if you prefer not to use any colourants, your work will likely have to do without the colour blue. Unless you are prepared to boil down red cabbage leaves.

MUST HAVE

A decent juicer is a must. With a good machine you can extract the best colourants from vegetables and fruit! Add an intense colour to juices by boiling them down into syrup. Think of: carrots, brambles, berries, beetroot, yellow carrots, or watermelon....

THE JAPANESE GARDEN

A thing that also works well is, instead of creating one single canvas, bringing several smaller canvases together to form one big one. That way, guests can take the painting apart, eat from it, and then put the end result back together. Make thirty small canvases carrying sashimi, beetroot crisps and sesame paste. This painting is inspired by a picture of a Japanese garden in autumn.

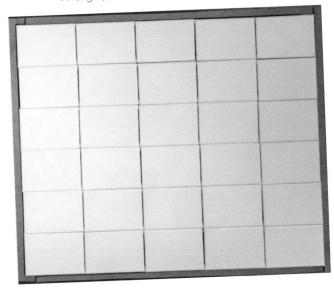

Arrange 30 small canvases in a panel.

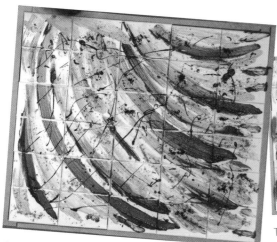

OK, now the black sesame paste, a bit of squid ink and Kikkoman soy sauce.

Time for graffiti, working with spray cans of edible paint. A bit of red, a bit of blue.

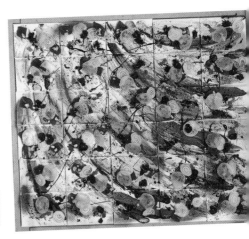

And now the shiso leaves, pieces of ginger, rettich, chioggia beet and finely cut Nori sheets. Add sashimi of hamachi tuna and edible flowers, such as fuchsias.

A little bit of paint over here, some over there, a drop of cucumber paint... Don't think, just do it!

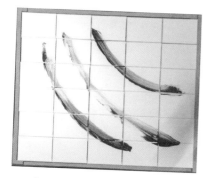

Start with stripes of spinach paint and a dollop of wasabi. Then use paint made out of beetroot and paint made out of turmeric and sesame oil.

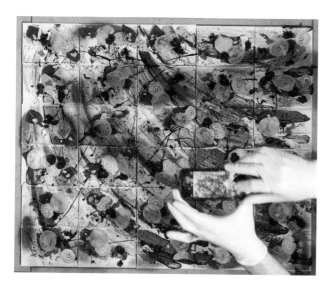

To finish off: a snapshot for social media!

INGREDIENTS

> **30 painter's canvases of 13 by 17 cm**
> *You can also replace these by 30 flat, rectangular plates.*
> **Spinach paint**
> *Made with 200 ml spinach (from a slow juicer), a tablespoon of wasabi and 10 grams agar. Heat the juice up to 60 degrees and add the agar. Mix in the wasabi and let it cool off. As soon as it has solidified, blend it in the food processor until it becomes a paint-like substance.*
> **Beetroot paint**
> *Do the same as with the spinach paint, but then using beetroot juice.*
> **Turmeric paint**
> *Do the same as with the spinach paint, but use 200 ml milk with 1 tbsp. of turmeric powder and 1 tbsp. of sesame oil.*
> **Cucumber paint**
> *Do the same as with the spinach paint, but then using cucumber juice.*
> **Squid ink**
> *Fresh squid ink is available at the fish vendor.*
> **Kikkoman soy sauce paint**
> *Made from 200 ml Kikkoman soy sauce and 10 grams agar.*
> *The rest of the processing is the same as with the spinach paint.*
> **Edible paint from a spray can**
> *Sold at the wholesaler or at a confectioner.*
> **Black sesame paste**
> **Shiso**
> *Beautiful leaves with a typical Eastern taste, reminiscent of cumin.*
> **Ginger**
> *Pickled ginger, as is served with sushi.*
> **Rettich**
> *You can cut wonderful shapes from this. Be careful to cut it very thinly, as it will otherwise dominate the entire dish.*
> **Chioggia beet**
> *Cut very thinly with the use of a mandoline. You can best place these on the painting raw.*
> **Nori**
> *As it is used for sushi.*
> **Tuna**
> *Ask the fish vendor for hamachi. This is a sustainable variant.*
> *If they do not have it, use organic salmon.*
> **Fuchsias**
> *These are difficult to find, but sometimes the wholesaler sells them.*

TIP: visit an ecological garden and ask for organic fuchsias.

CREATIVE CHEF'S GALLERY

Sweets Dots
Creative Chef and Marjon Hogervorst, 2013.
Materials: Vegetable and fruit, photographic
print on linen.

Selected Flower
Creative Chef and Rogier Boogaard, 2014.
Materials: Flowers, photographic print on
aluminium.

Veggie Squares
Creative Chef and Marjon Hogervorst, 2013.
Materials: Vegetable and fruit, photographic print
on aluminium.

A hard day's work
Creative Chef and Marjon Hogervorst, 2014.
Materials: Flowers, photographic print on
aluminium.

DUTCH MASTERS

Why would anyone want to hang up a painting of a platter of oysters? What's so great about a few depicted cheeses? In the Netherlands, the Golden Age was a time of much painting action. Every possible and impossible subject was painted. There were specialists for any imaginable painting genre and there were many fine art enthusiasts. The richer Dutch population would hang their houses, including their stables, full with paintings.

Still Life with a Gilt Cup
Willem Claesz. Heda, 1635

STILL LIFE

The word *still life* emerged around 1650 for depictions of things that stand still or have no life in them. The genre was not invented in the Netherlands, but nowhere else did it flourish as much as there. And this had a lot to do with the prosperity of the country in those days. Since the 16th century, the international trade had grown incredibly. Dutch ships sailed across the entire world, but by far the majority of their trade occurred inside of Europe. People also travelled more. Sons from rich families visited Paris and Rome, and artists also started exploring Europe looking for new subjects for their work.

A consequence of this international traffic was that people got acquainted with delicacies from faraway places. Oranges, lemons, olives and other exotic products were available in the Republic at rare intervals and for a great deal of money. Precisely because these products were expensive and exclusive, they made excellent subjects for paintings. One of the predecessors to the still life was the kitchen scene. This term was used for paintings with richly filled kitchens with vegetables, fruits, meats and poultry. These depictions almost always showed someone doing something with the ingredients, and in the background you would usually see a biblical story. This would often be the story of *Christ in the House of Martha*, in which Martha comes walking out of

Sumptuous Still Life
Adriaen van Utrecht, 1644

Still Life with Cheese
Floris Claesz. van Dijck, circa 1615

the kitchen to ask her sister Mary to come help her, while Mary just listens to Jesus. With this scene the painting depicts the contradiction between the active, earthly life and the contemplative, spiritual life. In later still lifes the biblical part was left out, but many people in the 17th century will have imagined it to be there. The more earthly wealth there was, the greater the danger one might lose sight of the higher realms. On the other hand, a still life was also simply a demonstration of skillful painting. We often see large roemers and splendid silver platters filled with oysters. Those all did an excellent job at showing how skillful the painter was at the art of depiction. At the same time, we are carried away to a more beautiful world in which various delicacies are on display. It is almost as though we only need to extend our arm out through the frame to grab some of it. Painters were well aware of this and tried to enforce this effect. Pay attention to how often you will see a plate balancing on the edge of a table. It invites you to take a second to push it back, lest it fall.
In the Netherlands, an incredible number of still lifes were made, and museums all over the world exhibit beautiful examples of these. For instance, why not pay a visit to the Rijksmuseum, the Mauritshuis or the Frans Hals Museum? After all, there is no alternative to enjoying them in real life.

- Carel Huydecoper

Check out the edible still life paintings on the following pages

MATERIALS

> *A roemer glass*
> *A fruit peeler*
> *Extra boards for propping*
> *Lace cloths*
> *Grapes, many grapes*
> *Old knives with those characteristic ivory handles*
> *Nuts and dried fruit: perfect for filling*
> *Vine leaves, fake will also do!*
> *Kitschy crockery from the thrift shop*
> *If possible, a lamp that you can shine straight at the front*
> *A nameplate with title details, in order to complete the picture*

How do you make an edible still life?

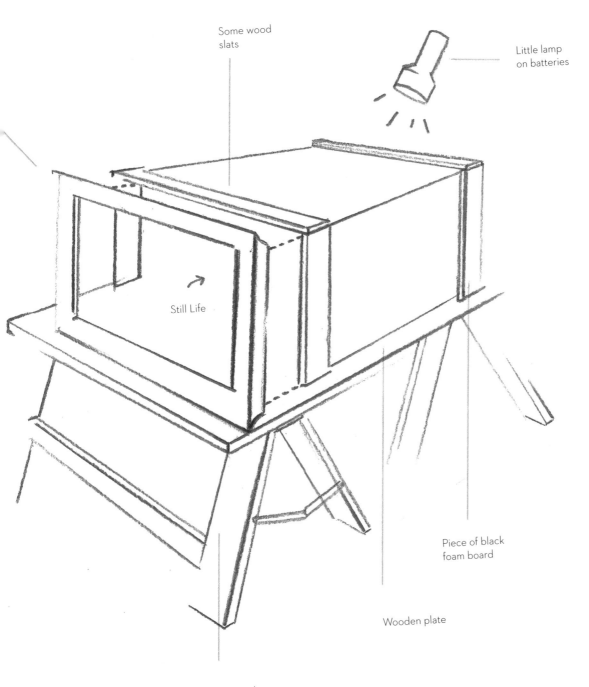

Some wood slats

Little lamp on batteries

Still Life

Piece of black foam board

Wooden plate

Workbenches

Recipe for a pretty picture

VENUS ON YOUR PLATE

Of course, you can also make a dish inspired by an existing painting. For instance, the Birth of Venus by Botticelli. A symbol of beauty and eroticism. Venus, born from the foam of the sea, looks at us with an innocent glance. Serve the image with the dish.

> **1 tbsp. butter**
> **1 scallop**
  Fry the scallop in the soft butter.
> **Seaweed**
  During the frying, throw in the seaweed for the salty taste.
> **1 tsp. cacao powder**
  Sprinkle over the scallop.
> **2 oysters**
  Collect the juice of the oysters and chop the meat finely.
> **2 oyster leaves**
  Place some seaweed and oyster leaves in an empty scallop shell and add the scallop on top.
> **Sevruga caviar**
> **Gold leaf**
  Add a spoon of caviar and some gold leaf on top of it.
> **5 cl champagne**
  Mix the champagne with the oyster liquid and foam it up with a hand blender.

Finish with the foam of the sea!

THE CHEF IS
THE SCRIPTWRITER.
THE HOST. THE DIRECTOR.
THE PLATE IS
THE STAGE.

AND THE INGREDIENTS
THE ACTORS.
WAITERS DANCE.

THE TABLE DECORATIONS
FORM THE SETTING.
THE WINE. THE MUSIC.
EACH COURSE AN ACT.

WELCOME TO THE THEATRE OF TASTE!

INGREDIENTS

... they make up an important part of your food experience. Always use good ingredients, preferably from local and reliable suppliers. Behind all these products you'll find beautiful stories, which you can tell while serving your dinner. Dedicate all your efforts, search the internet, collect fun facts and make it personal.

Flower Power

One of the most powerful ingredients that add a true food experience to your dish are edible flowers. Especially if you pick them yourself. And you'd be surprised to know how many flowers and herbs there are, many of which most of us haven't even heard of, much less tasted!

PICKING YOUR INGREDIENTS YOURSELF

This is educational, fun and delicious. And with any luck, you'll have the Creative Chef nearby to transform the things you've picked into a delightful meal!
But you can also do that yourself. Be curious, read books on herbs and edible plants, and visit as many gardens as possible. A whole world will reveal itself to you and you can start harvesting your own food!

VISIT A GARDEN

Enjoy the smell. Take a tour, pick fresh strawberries or juicy plums, and just think of nothing!

Poppies are a suitable replacement for lettuce leaves.
Great for a dinner with your loved one!

The colour blue of the cornflower is unique in nature. The taste is negligible.

Delicious, the garden cosmos, but you can only eat its leaves.

Tree onions are delightful for grilling and serving with sea salt and melted butter.

Carnations are nice for adding some colour to your dish. *Only eat the flower's leaves.*

Lucky clovers work well with fish; they have a pleasant sour taste.

Nasturtium has a nice and spicy taste. You can eat the flowers and the leaves!

What is more wonderful than dining in your own garden?

Dining with self-picked ingredients !

A DINNER
FROM THE GARDEN AND IN
THE GARDEN

Do you have a beautiful garden or do you know a nice place? Go there and cook for your friends. But first take some time to pick those ingredients. Put your guests to work for the dessert. Let them enjoy picking from the garden, while you set the table and prepare the drinks. As soon as they start on the entrée, you can get started with preparing dessert!

First pick those ingredients. Educational, fun and delicious.

There, the guests are taken care of... Let me now
make something divine out of this rhubarb.

RHUBARB

*with strawberries and a bit of honey with yoghurt,
fennel herb and lemon verbena.*

RHUBARB COMPOTE

> **3 stalks of rhubarb**
> **50 grams of honey**
> **1 bunch of fennel herb**
  *Cut the rhubarb into pieces and place on the fire
  with water, honey and fennel herb.*

STRAWBERRIES

> **250 grams of strawberries**
> **Dessert wine**
> **Bunch of fennel herb**
> **Bunch of lemon verbena**

*Cut the crowns of the strawberries. Save the crowns in a saucepan
and pour the dessert wine over it with finely chopped lemon verbena
and fennel herb. Add some honey and let the mixture boil down very
slowly until it becomes a thin syrup. Let it cool off. Cut the strawberries
into pieces and mix them through the syrup. In the meantime, let the
rhubarb cool off. It needs to have become a kind of rough jam.*

SERVE

> **Jar of honey**
> **50 grams of Greek yoghurt**
  *Place the rhubarb on a small plate. Add the strawberries on top and
  finish off with yoghurt, branches of fennel herb and a stripe of honey.
  Wow, so good!*

Bad weather?
Just harvest indoors!

How can you create an indoor picking sensation? Visit a garden store and pick up a few planters with fresh herbs and young lettuce. Place these on the table so that the guests can pick their own salad at the table!

OR

Place a complete greenhouse and give the guests a shopping list. They can use the list to pick the right necessities, after which you turn those into something delicious! Super Fresh, right?

CREATIVE CHEF'S 'SEIZE THE DAY' TIPS

> *With these tips your day cannot go wrong!*
> *Start your morning by making breakfast for someone and put on a playlist by Creative Chef!*
> *Take an alternative route to work, stop by a local greengrocer that you haven't visited before and buy your lunch there, plus an apple for someone at work who you actually never get to talk to.*
> *Give that person - who you usually never talk to - the apple.*
> *During lunch, invite everyone at work to your home for a barbecue that same evening and ask everyone to bring something in terms of drink, food or barbecue essentials.*
> *Before going to sleep, read from this book; then you'll have made my day, too!*

Flower salad

SALAD

- > Nasturtium, leaves and flowers
- > Fuchsia
- > Corn shoots
- > Wood violets
- > Forget-me-nots
- > Carnation
- > Leaf lettuce

DRESSING

- > Prosecco, 1 tablespoon
- > Orange blossom water, 1 teaspoon
- > Tarragon mustard, 1 tablespoon
- > Apricot coulis, 1 tablespoon
- > Juice of 1 lime
- > Extra virgin olive oil

Pick the flowers in an ecological garden or grow them yourself!
Mix them carefully and arrange the salad on a plate. Make a dressing
from the Prosecco, orange blossom water, tarragon mustard, apricot
coulis and lime juice. Mix all ingredients with a hand blender or a whisk,
if necessary. Then stir in the extra virgin olive oil until the dressing
shows a nice binding.

SERVING TIP

- > **Scent**
  Perfume No. 1
- > **Sound**
  Flower, performed by Amos Lee
- > **Occasion**
  Why not serve a flower salad once instead
  of giving a bunch of flowers?
- > **Truly original**
  Wrap the salad in cellophane and give
  during a drinks gathering as a bunch of
  flowers.
- > **Tip**
  Make the dressing shortly in advance,
  so that it still contains the bubbles of the
  Prosecco!

DIY–
Herb Tea Bar

Have picnic, high tea or fun lunch coming up? Make a
Do-It-Yourself Herb Tea bar. Prepare a selection of fresh
herbs such as lemon verbena, peppermint, various types
of mint and tarragon. Place a jar of honey and a kettle
next to it! That's it; you're good to go...

Fennel Herb

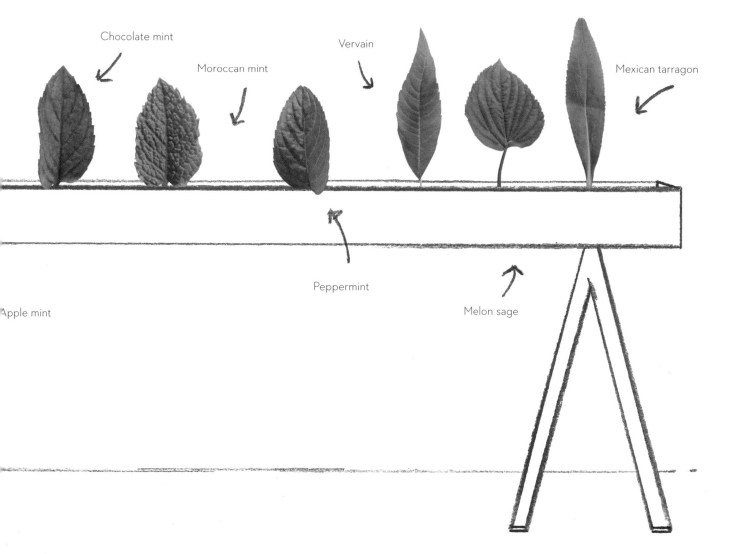

Chocolate mint

Moroccan mint

Vervain

Mexican tarragon

Peppermint

Apple mint

Melon sage

CREATIVE CHEF'S PINTXOGRAPHIC

Step-by-step plan for the coolest sandwich with a dish on top and a skewer through it (= pintxo)!

How does it work? Choose your favourite from each list and combine. Or turn it into a game! Take three or more dice and each time you throw, choose an ingredient from the list that coincides with the number you threw.

A PINTXO BY THE CREATIVE CHEF:

1

MEAT NOR FISH
> Halloumi cheese
> Seaweed
> Chicken from the vegetarian butcher
> Goat cheese
> Quail egg
> Roasted beetroot
> Blue cheese
> Époisses de Bourgogne
> Chard
> White beans
> Burrata Pugliese
> Red berries
> Apple

2

SOMETHING SENSATIONAL
> Edible flowers
> Hop shoots
> Freeze-dried vegetable
> Fresh stevia
> Fern tops
> Vegetables from your own garden
> Honeycomb
> Black sesame paste
> Rainbow chard
> Deventer black chard
> Vegetable crisps
> Brillat-Savarin cheese
> Flower sprouts
> Basil flower

3

SOMETHING QUIRKY
> A card with a message
> Fries
> Bitterbal (savoury Dutch meat-based snack)
> Sushi
> Serve something with headphones and music
> Wrap the pintxo as a gift
> Serve with a speech balloon
> Serve with name plates
> Serve on an edible painting
> Use a pipette

2. *Something special, such as edible honeycomb*

4. *Something delicious, such as blue cheese*

5. *Lettuce leaf to use as a base to keep moisture away from your sandwich*

1. A pintxo: Spanish word for Skewer

3. Something decorative like a scoop of watermelon

6. A tasty piece of bread

4

SOMETHING WITH FRAGRANCE OR COLOUR

> Use the stink-o-meter *(on page 138)*
> Use a scented candle
> Make use of essential oils
> Melt ice cubes of hydrophilic fragrances *(on page 134)*
> Use colourants
> Chioggia beetroot
> Carrots in various colours
> Japanese radish
> Smoked sprat
> Tomato caviar
> Edible flowers

+

5

WHAT ON EARTH!?

> Deep-fried calf's brains
> Salad of tarragon mayonnaise and mealworms
> Frog legs
> Sevruga caviar
> Fried grasshoppers
> Roasted chicken skins
> Pig's tongue
> Rabbit kidneys
> Accompanied by a drink in a water gun
> Edible gold leaf
> Beef Kalashnikov
> Fried blood sausage

+

6

MEAT AND FISH

> Steak tartare
> Dry sausage
> Pâté
> Slow-braised beef
> Prawns
> Salmon sashimi
> Shrimp croquette
> Quail legs
> Cockles
> Mussels
> Saddle of lamb
> Serrano ham
> Scallop

Name your pintxo

THE TWIN BROTHER

MS CONTINENTAL

ESSY ELEANOR HENK

ODYSSEUS

ELMO GREENSTAR

HARRY LAMB

JACOB SEVRUGA

**MELVIN JOHANNES KOKKEL
WELLINGTON**

JIMI

MR BUNN

SIR CRUNCH-A-LOT

HENRI BALL

GILMORE KATEY RICARDO   VITTORIO   MR PINK

it's juice time

JUICY JUICE RECIPES FOR FESTIVAL-GOERS

Considering that there are thousands of possibilities for making juices with a slow juice machine and vegetable, herbs, types of fruit, coconut milk, oil, nuts and dairy - the prospects can be quite dizzying, don't you think? Creative Chef loves serving juices at festivals.

THE LIQUID JOINT

> 2 apples
> 2 sprigs of mint
> 1 branch of lemon verbena
> 10 cl hemp juice
> Chopped vegetables for stirring

Put the apple together with the mint into the juicer. Collect in a cup and pour the hemp juice in with it.
Stir for a moment with a piece of carrot and serve with ice, if so desired. For as far as I know, hemp juice is only available through its only supplier in the world: Sana Hemp Juice.

STRAWBERRY DELIGHT

> 1 apple
> 100 grams of strawberries
> 100 grams of cucumber
> 50 grams of fennel
> Chopped vegetables for stirring

Put the apple with the strawberries, the cucumber and the fennel into the juicer and collect the juice in a cup. Stir for a moment with a piece of cucumber and serve with flowers from the liquorice plant and some ice.

ANTI-HANGOVER WATER

> 1 apple
> 50 grams of cucumber
> 50 grams of carrots
> 50 grams raspberries
> 50 grams strawberries
> 10 cl Ouzo (Greek anise liquor)
> 1 knife tip wasabi
> 1 cherry
> Chopped vegetable for stirring

Put the apple, the cucumber, the carrots, the raspberries, the strawberries and the wasabi into juicer and collect the juice in a cocktail shaker containing the Ouzo and some crushed ice. Shake and serve in a glass with a cherry in it and a stirrer made from a stalk of celery.

Setting a table and eating at a table is actually quite boring. Serving a tray with snacks, too. Why not create an Experience Bar! Your guests will be taken on a journey through time at your bar: stories, products and – most importantly – your inspiring passion for your food and the ingredients it contains!

THE FOOD PHARMACIST

Your own live food experience in the form of
The Food Pharmacist. What that is? Well, you tell
your guests stories about extraordinary products
that are extremely healthy. About flavours the guests
have never tasted before, and special cocktails,
crazy products and healing herbal tea are brought
into the mix to offer the guests an enjoyable and
informative experience of the quality of mother
nature's stuff – straight from our Food Pharmacy!

What will you do: you brew healthy elixirs that would boggle the mind
of any regular pharmacist! You take your guests on a roller coaster ride
of flavours and an ultimate taste explosion that contains all aspects:
presentation, information, association, time, scent, sound and location.

WTF
is
happening
?!

Healthy elixirs that would boggle the mind of any regular pharmacist!

WTF IS HAPPENING?!

A 10 -COURSE MENU TO IMPROVE YOUR PARTY

Okay, how can you go about this? Thoroughly read up on the material and make sure that you are able to tell a good story. Make a joke now and then and try to take people along with you in your narrative.

1

CHAMPAGNE HERB

While your guests chew, you explain to them that this is a palate cleanser to reset their taste, as it will soon begin: the *roller coaster* ride of biodiversity and flavour!

MOSTARDA DI CREMONA

Crazy, isn't it? This is fruit pickled in a syrup of mustard seed! What does it taste like?

ROASTED GRASSHOPPER

Grasshopper is the nutty taste I was referring to! And what do you think? Is it savoury, sweet or everything at the same time? What does it remind you of?

2

EDIBLE HONEYCOMB

While you hand this out, you explain that this is virgin honeycomb, which means that you can eat the wax. You picked it up fresh from the beekeeper this morning!

3

FENNEL FLOWER

While your guests chew on their honeycomb, you hand them a piece of fennel flower. Notice how it starts tasting like honey liquorice? Honey also goes well with nuts!

OYSTER LEAF

Oysters! Isn't that cool? All right, on to the *grand finale!*

ICE WATER

Spray some ice water in the face of your guests and put a blindfold on them. Say: "Imagine you are in a pine forest in Siberia" and place headphones with Cossack music on their head (check our playlists).

BLOODY CATHARINA

Massage the shoulders and serve a Bloody Catharina, a cocktail of:

ICE-COLD

> 1 part vodka
> 1 part gazpacho or tomato juice
> 1 tablespoon tomato caviar

WARM

> Beetroot foam with porcini powder

SCENT OF PINE FOREST

Spray Creative Chef's perfume No. 3 with Pine Forest Scent under the nose of your guest.

TO FINISH

A knife tip of wasabi!

MICRO-ADVENTURE

Have you ever heard of a micro-adventure? No?
Well, it's simply something crazy that you need
to do sometimes to spice up your life a bit. Micro-
adventures can be anything: sleeping in the garden
for a night, shadowing a baker for a day, holding a
speech during your afternoon lunch break.

Here you'll find some cards that you can serve @ random with finger
food. It makes for a fun way to liven up the gathering!

PS I would give the cards that instruct the guest to kiss the chef to the
guest(s) you like the most!

*If you just received a hug from someone,
go to the women's toilet. You will find an
envelope there. If you don't, then go back
in ten minutes.*

*Your time starts... now!
Within one hour, give four
heartfelt compliments to four
different people.*

Shout BINGO really loudly.

*If you are a woman,
go to the kitchen and
give the chef a kiss.
If not, by all means
continue as you were!*

*If you have received this
card and you are reading
this, embrace the person
closest to you.*

Grab your telephone and start holding it up in the air for a while until you receive an envelope. Then pass it on to someone who gives you a compliment.

Head towards the chest as soon as you've heard the word 'eagle eye'. Grab the envelope from the chest and bring it to the first person you see with a telephone in his or her hand.

Head over to the person who calls out BINGO and talk to him or her. Make sure you get that envelope.
Then call:
06 ....
Agree to meet at the entrance and hand over the envelope.

Tell two people about your collection of stamps from the previous century. You don't actually have one, but let your imagination do the work.

Run outside and loudly shout the code word *Eagle Eye.*

SCE

Smell triggers the imagination!

Smell is one of the most fun and important aspects to complete a food experience. Scents can make your guests' mouths water. Smell evokes memories and can help trigger the imagination.

EDIBLE PERFUME

All right, you now know that smell is one of the most important aspects in tasting food. After all, when you have a cold you don't taste anything, do you? Well, what if you could serve a scent that contributes to the food experience? A scent that evokes memories and associations to amplify the food experience. For instance, think of a typically Mediterranean smell with a Mediterranean dish! Or your favourite scent with a delicious dish, which you remember from the past.

WE'VE GOT IT!

The ultimate recipe for edible perfume. A perfume on the basis of hydrophiles. Not on the basis of alcohol, essential oil and fats, as is common with perfumes and eau de cologne. It works best to spray on hot dishes, as the liquid then evaporates.

WHAT ARE HYDROPHILES?

Hydrophiles are liquid by-products from extraction of essential oils. The best-known used in the kitchen are orange blossom water and rose water. Those give many North-African dishes their typical taste.

AND WHAT ABOUT ESSENTIAL OILS?

You can also use those! Please note: inquire whether they are 100% natural oils. Only then are they suitable for use. In addition, you cannot mix them together very well or use them in watery substances. As you might know, water and oil do not go together!

TIPS

> The bottle needs to have dark glass, so you can store it for a long time.

> The bottleneck should have a dropper cap.

> Always store the essential oil out of reach of children.

> Store in a cool and securely closed place.

> The quality of essential oils will gradually decrease; it remains usable for one to two years.

> Freeze your hydrophyles into ice cubes and melt them above a candle. That will create a delightful scent!

> There is a great difference in quality of essential oils. Cheap essential oil is often synthetic. So do not use these!

> Essential oils work best in dressings with a scent, sprayed from hydrophiles.

NO. 1

Parfum Méditerrané

> White balsamic vinegar
> Basil
> Lavender water
> Rosemary water
> Cornflower water
> Sage
> Tomato consommé
> Verbena water
> Herbal vinegar
> Garlic

Mix the ingredients and pour it all into an old perfume bottle. Then serve with for instance lamb neck cooked in lavender with tomato confit and aubergine caviar.

NO. 2

Flower Power

> Camomile water
> Verbena water
> Linden blossom water
> Rose water

Delightful scent to go with a flower salad! Close your eyes and imagine that you are standing in a field of flowers under a blossoming linden tree!

FUN PERFUME FACTS

The Egyptians were the first to use perfume for their personal pleasure, but the production remained a privilege reserved for priests. Only they were allowed to occupy themselves with the perfumery. To this end, temples used to contain a specially equipped laboratory. Much later, kings and queens were also allowed to make use of the perfumes.

NO. 3

From Russia, with love

- **Witch Hazel**
- **Pine scent**
- **Juniper**
- **Vodka**

Nice smell for with vodka and beetroot! Close your eyes and imagine that you are standing in a Russian pine forest!

NO. 4

Fresh & Tonka

- **Hyssop water**
- **Yarrow water**
- **Peppermint water**
- **One Tonka bean**

This scent goes well with chocolate dishes! Perhaps because it quickly evokes an association with mint chocolate.

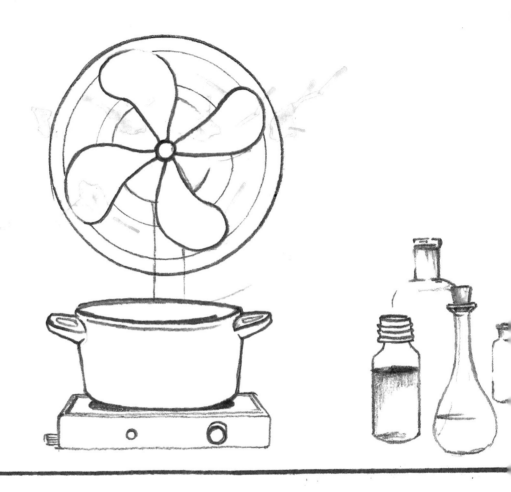

THE SCENT DJ

Great to try out. Place a scent-DJ booth in the room during a dinner.
Create a collection of scents. Think of:

> *Orange blossom water*
> *Rose water*
> *Sandalwood*
> *Strawberries*
> *Cinnamon*
> *Star anise*
> *Fennel seed*
> *Edible perfumes*

Heat these substances in a saucepan and place a fan behind it.

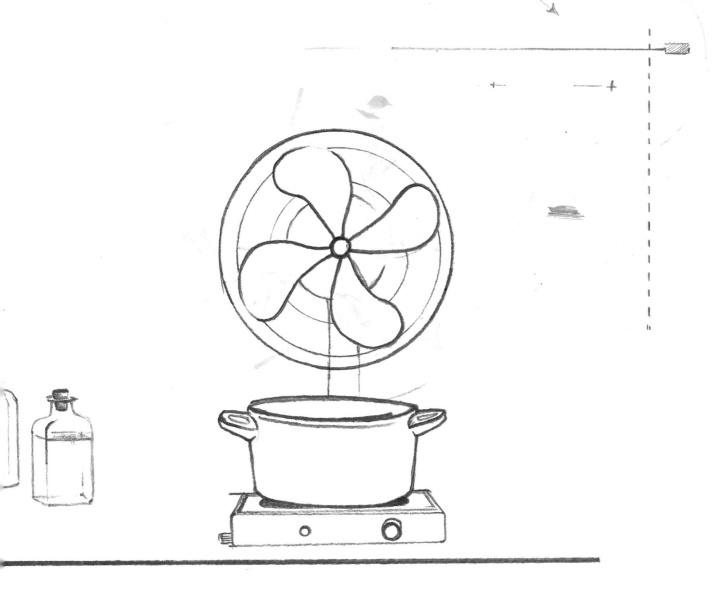

We take requests!

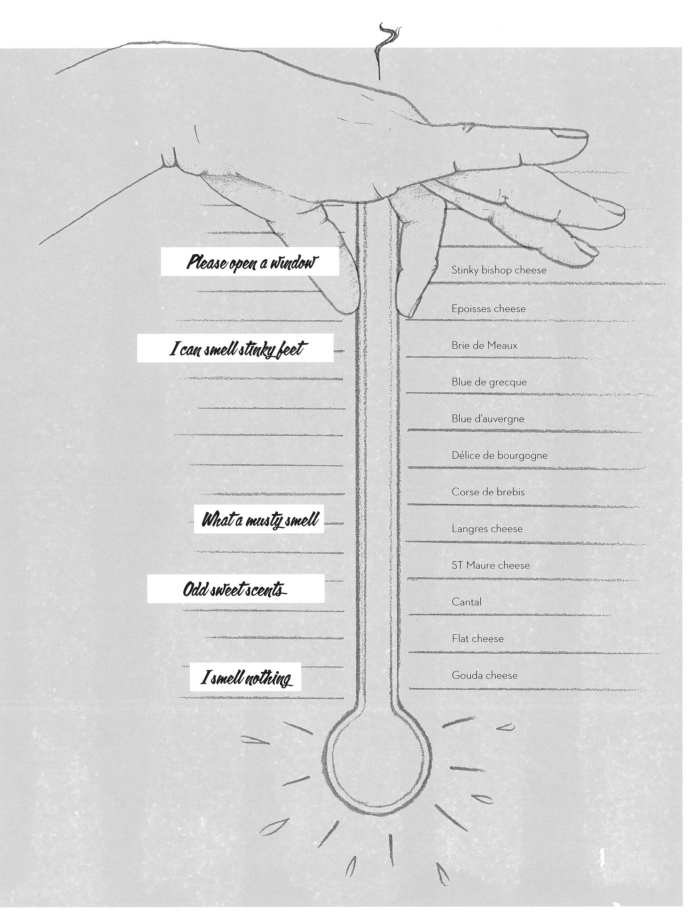

Please open a window

I can smell stinky feet

What a musty smell

Odd sweet scents

I smell nothing

Stinky bishop cheese

Epoisses cheese

Brie de Meaux

Blue de grecque

Blue d'auvergne

Délice de bourgogne

Corse de brebis

Langres cheese

ST Maure cheese

Cantal

Flat cheese

Gouda cheese

SAY CHEESE

Read this text while you serve your fragrant
composition of cheese to your guests.
Tip: raise your voice a bit and do it with lots
of melody and liveliness!

A CACOPHANY OF STINKY CHEESES

*(free interpretation of Emile Zola's cheese symphony and the Dutch
translation by Bart van Loo)*

My god, how these cheeses reek! They stink so delightfully that it surprises
my nose, so to speak!

I'm thinking of a bombastic music composition, consisting of an Orchestra
of various instruments. Bass sounds of a gargantuan Emmentaler, flanked
by its brothers from Gruyère. Or aromatic brass force of thick white mould
cheeses with a dash of musical flair. Princely altos such as the Roqueforts
reach everyone's nose as a perfume of temptation; so marbled and fat as
they are, so fragrant are they, so do they reek of venom! And while the Brie
Brethren gloriously continue to turn mouldy and their creamy substances
expand, a breeze of stables, shoes and other smelly sounds blows by. It
is probably the English cheddars that crack the high notes. Or instead,
maybe it's the truly stinky cheeses that lead us to the grand finale.

Light-yellow Mont d'Ors with their sweet notes or the disgusting Troyes
with their stinky stanks. The humid cellar fragrance of the Camemberts and
the wry smells of the Neufchatels and the Maroilles. Together the Pont-
l'Évêque and red-hued Livarots form a nauseating, yet pleasant melody that
finally reaches its pedal point with the repulsively reeking Olivet, wrapped
in nut leaves, as a true cacophony of stink that settles in your nostrils and
makes you long for a harmonious final chord in your mouth.

Oh, how these cheeses reek. Oh, how these cheeses reek.

Let your cheese platter tell a story!

Use the speech balloons on this page to spruce up your cheese platter. If you stick them to pieces of carton or foam board, they will easily stay upright. Otherwise, you can simply lay them down. Incidentally, you can also easily expand the repertoire yourself with your own speech balloons.

Tip
Write some personal jokes about yourself and your guests on the speech balloon.

je Stinkt

Say Cheeese

TING

The environment of the place where the dish comes from, but also where you eat it, has a strong effect on your food experience! And if you then think of the fact that environments can evoke various associations with other worlds and other times, the possibilities become dizzying, don't they?

Bring the environment of origin to the plate!

Camouflage Carpaccio

VEGGIE'S NIGHTMARE

> **400 grams washed spinach**
> **1 cucumber**
   Use the juice extractor to make spinach juice and cucumber juice.
> **Squid ink**
   *Colour half of the cucumber juice with some squid ink. You now
   have three colours of juice. Light green, dark green and black.*
> **100 grams tenderloin, thinly sliced**
> **Parmesan cheese**
> **Ripe avocado**
> **Balsamic vinegar**
> **Sea salt**

Place the Carpaccio of tenderloin on the plates.
*Also add some flakes of Parmesan cheese and avocado. Finish with
balsamic vinegar and sea salt.*
Mix the three liquids with agar according to the instructions on the package.
*Pour one liquid at a time onto the Carpaccio and ensure that you create a
nice camouflage colour pattern.*
*If all goes well, the agar will ensure that the liquids will solidify into a
gelatine-like substance. Place a soldier figurine on the plate and you
are done.*

Add a toy soldier and
you are ready to go.

For accompaniment on your plate. To increase your food experience

Pizza Vesuvio

Meatball

Christmas biscuits

Ranch burger

Sandwich with cheddar

Raclette

Vodka martini, shaken not stirred

Favourite food from your childhood

Granita

Wild boar sausage

Chilli con Carne

Line-caught sea bass

Grandmother's kitchen

Cheese fondue

Fruits de mer

Glass of milk

Deep-sea mussels

Bouillabaisse

Snow eggs

Cheese platter

Champagne with strawberries and whipped cream

An edible beach!

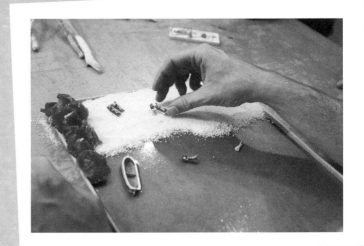

How can I create a beach to eat up?

AN EDIBLE BEACH

It's the midst of summer and it's raining! You want to go to the beach, but the weather gods are not working with you... Don't worry, just create your own beach at the table and spend some time Creative Cheffing at home!

THE SEAWATER

> Silver- or white-coloured bowl with open edges
> Agar
> White wine
> Fresh seaweed
> Mussels
> Lemongrass
> Blue colourant

Make a broth on intuition using the ingredients listed above. It should have a clear hint of the sea! Mix the agar according to the ratios indicated on the package and pour everything onto the platter. Leave to solidify and, right before it has fully hardened, place some little boats in the sea.

THE SAND

> Panko
> Anchovies
> Sesame seeds

For a briny effect, bake the panko in a frying pan in the oil of the can anchovies and, if so desired, add the sesame seeds during the frying. Sprinkle the sand onto the water.

FOR THE SASHIMI

> Your own choice of fresh fish

FURTHERMORE

> Cockles and clams
> Edible types of seaweed
> Shells
> Model boats
> Mini-visitors
> Sea sounds

Use these ingredients to finish the whole.

THE GINGERBREAD HOUSE

Build your dream house from gingerbread! You can literally serve your dream environment and eat it.

What you need to do:

> *Contact an architectural firm, ask for a design drawing and discuss your wishes. I had this done by my Dutch friends Peter Popke de Jong and Pieter Koningsveld of USE architects.*
> *Wait for the design drawing to be finished.*
> *Buy a large amount of biscuits.*
> *Buys lots of cake.*
> *Instead of cement, you use chocolate.*
> *Use a tape measure, so that the proportions are aligned with the drawing.*
> *All right, time to build. This is quite tricky, but it will give you an idea how tricky it is to building your own dream house in reality, too. Consider it a challenge!*

Result: you get to eat your own dream house!

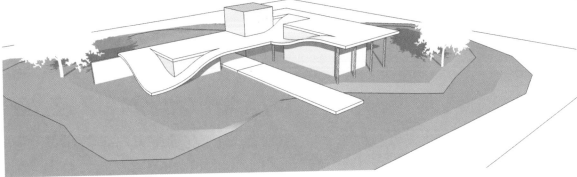

Breaking down
the house together
and encountering new
tastes as you
go along!

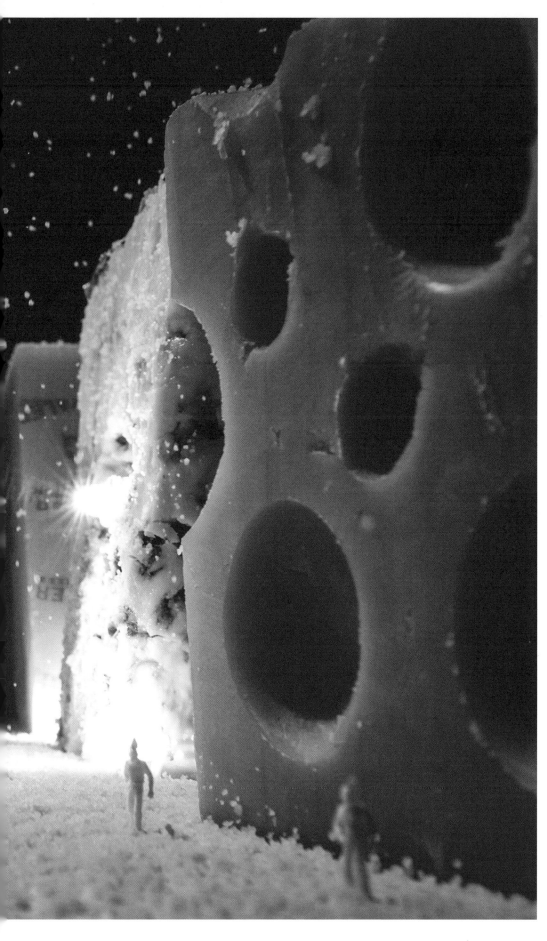

NY CHEESE

Creative Chef, Reinier Suurenbroek
and Wouter de Winter, 2013
Materials: Cheese, photographic
print on aluminium.
Items: 50, numbered.

Stories and how they are told
form one of the most important
factors that influence your food
experience.

Put a story in
your dish!

★ BIEFSTUK KALASHNIKOV ★

Chicken Marengo

Napoleon stands by himself in from of his tent and looks out over the fray. At the appropriate distance his adjudants nervously wait for instructions. No one breathes a word.

Everything points towards the impending defeat of the French army. The Austrian supremacy is simply too great. The officers behind the slight figure are all thinking the same: what will Napoleon do? Is there anything he can do?

All of a sudden: trumpets. French trumpets! From a nearby forest a long row of French soldiers come marching towards them. At the head of the troop, general Desaix arrives and kneels before Napoleon. "This battle is lost," he says.

The sense of everyone's defeat is almost tangible. Discouragement daunts on them. Until Desaix continues speaking: "But it's only two o' clock in the afternoon. There's still time to win a second battle today!" Loud cheers emerge among the French officers.

"Long live France!" Desaix shouts and heads into battle with his soldiers.

Napoleon turns around. "I'm hungry," he says. The chef is summoned at once. But there seems to be a problem: the supplies are depleted.

Napoleon is hungry

"One chicken, some crayfish, a few eggs and tomatoes," the chef whispers agitated, "herbs, garlic and olive oil. What on earth can I do with those?"

"Think of something, chef! Napoleon is hungry." The chef stomps off and disappears into the kitchen. The minutes tick away excruciatingly slowly. The adjudants hardly dare to look at one another. That darn chef will figure out something, won't he? Eventually the chef reappears, the dish in his shaky hands. As soon as the plate is placed before him, Napoleon looks at it with raised eyebrows. Carefully, a tiny bite disappears into his mouth. Napoleon chews... swallows... The tension can be cut with a knife. Then: "Délicieux!"

And while at a short distance the Austrian army is being defeated after all, Napoleon eats the dish that will always be linked to his name for the first time: Poulet Marengo.

Délicieux!

By Reinder Eekhof

POULET MARENGO

> **One whole chicken**
> **Olive oil**
> **Eggs**
> **Tomato**
> **White wine**
> **Crayfish**
> **Rosemary**
> **Garlic**
> **Onions**
> **Parsley**

Cut the chicken into equal parts and fry until golden brown. Add some broth, plus the chopped tomato, white wine, garlic, onions and rosemary. Leave to simmer softly for an hour. Serve the chicken on a platter and arrange nicely with the boiled eggs, crayfish and, if available, a tin soldier with a French uniform. Finish with olive oil and pepper and salt. Read the story to your guests before you serve the food!

Emperor Claudius and his women

Power eroticises, they say. Emperor Claudius of Rome didn't experience much of that. He was not lucky when it came to women and that is putting it mildly. Admittedly, Claudius was no Adonis. He had a limp, stuttered and was spastic. Many people thought he was retarded.

However, isn't love all about the inside? Apparently not. Women did not want anything to do with him. It already started with his own mother and grandmother publically making fun of his disabilities.

However, that was child's play compared to what Claudius would have to endure from his wives.

His first wife cheated on him. His second wife was not much better. But Claudius was truly unfortunate with his third wife: his second cousin Valeria Messalina. This Valeria couldn't get enough of 'it'. She worked as a prostitute in a Roman brothel on the side. One time she held a competition and 'served' 25 men in one day. For a long time, Claudius let Valeria go her horny way, but eventually enough was enough: he executed her.

Do you think Claudius was unlucky with his third wife, Valeria? Meet wife number four: Claudius' first cousin Julia Agrippina. She had Claudius adopt her son as heir to the throne and then had him killed. But at least in a culinary manner. She served Claudius his favourite dish of exquisite Caesar's mushrooms, through which she had mixed the incredibly poisonous mushroom Amanita Phalloides, known as the death cap. Fortunately for Claudius, this was exactly at a time that he was having heavy diarrhoea, which meant that the poison did not remain in his body long enough to cause any damage. But Julia Agrippina was persistent. Not long after, she succeeded at murdering Claudius after all and secured the position of Emperor of Rome for her son. She wasn't able to enjoy it for long: five years afterwards her own son killed her. His name: Nero.

Fatally delicious

By Reinder Eekhof

FVNGI FARNEI VEL BOLETI

Fungi Farnei; elixi calidi exsiccati in garo, piper accipiuntur, ita ut piper cum liquamine teres.

Creative Chef's version of above-mentioned abracadabra
> **Butter**
> **Wild mushrooms**
> **Garum (Roman version of fish sauce)**

Fry the mushrooms in the butter and add a tablespoon of fish sauce. Serve with skewers as a snack for with your drinks. Do not forget to read the story.

RECIPE FROM APICIUS

An old Roman writer of cookbooks and colleague from the time around the birth of Christ.

Like a god in France
Le Petit Couvert

A day out of the life of His Majesty Louis XIV, king of France, nicknamed 'the Sun King'.

08:00 am

Louis is woken by a chamberlain, who has waited all night at the footboard of His Majesty for that moment. Dressing occurs in the presence of 40 chosen noblemen. Louis chats away, while the others are not allowed to speak. His Majesty keeps breakfast sober: a few bowls of broth.

10:00 am

Holy service in the Royal Chapel. The choir sings a new piece, especially composed for Louis every day.

11:00 am

The king received ministers and foreign envoys in his cabinet.

12:00 pm

Louis visits his favourite ladies (not being the queen). He loves all women: peasant girls, chambermaids, daughters of the staff, and upper-class ladies.

1:00 pm

Lunch at Versailles is called Le Petit Couvert, although there is very little 'petit' about this meal. For instance, his lunch menu can consist of four different kinds of soup, stuffed pheasant, poultry, mutton, hams, boiled eggs, various salads and a plate full of cake,

Chatter and laughter are forbidden during dinner

fruit and jam. The light lunch variant, Le Très Petit Couvert, still consists of three courses, not to mention the excessive dessert as Louis loves sweets. Louis enjoys his lunch alone, seated at an enormous table in his bedroom.

2:00 pm
The afternoon programme changes and can involve for example matters of state, a walk through the gardens of Versailles, or a hunting party.

6:00 pm
For dinner His Majesty invites guests to come watch as he plays billiards or cards. This is followed up by a ball.

10:00 pm
The dinner is called Le Grand Couvert. Louis eats less than during lunch, but still samples from all forty dishes that are served. Chatter and laughter are forbidden during the dinner: His Majesty does not enjoy being distracted when he eats.

11:30 pm
Coucher (sleep), again a public ceremony.

01:00 am
End of the day.

By Reinder Eekhof

LOUIS THE 14TH

According to an example by a chef from that time: Francois Pierre, Sieur de la Varenne

FOIE DE VEAU SAUTE A LA LYONNAISE

> Calf's liver
> Knob of goose fat
> Chopped onion
> Glass of chicken broth
> 1 tablespoon of verjuice
> Slice of old bread, in crumbs
> Mushrooms and capers

Cut the calf's liver into thin slices. Add some goose fat in the frying pan and heat up. Fry the liver briefly and add onions, a bit of broth and some verjuice (or just vinegar). Do not fry for too long! Add some breadcrumbs to bind the sauce. Serve with fried mushrooms and capers.

ANGRY TOMATO RELISH

Grab six tomatoes and get really angry about something. Channel all your frustration in about six throws and smash those tomatoes with all your heart and soul. Collect the smashed tomatoes in an oven dish and add one tablespoon of brown sugar, one tablespoon of ginger syrup, one tablespoon of balsamic vinegar, one tablespoon of soy sauce, two tablespoons of olive oil and two tablespoons of finely grated onion. Make yourself angry again, and squash two cloves of garlic to add to the rest. Roast everything in ten minutes in the oven at 180 degrees and place all of it in the food processor. Blend fine and add pepper and salt to taste.

Serve the Angry Tomato Relish on your hamburger or on a cracker!

LET YOUR INGREDIENTS TELL A STORY!

Serve your dish on a piece of baking paper. If you do it well, you can also weave some of the origins of your ingredients and how they were prepared into your narrative.

7.
You are right, this is such a nice spot! Hey, flowers, aren't you enjoying this place too?

6.
I agree with the officer: you should always pay for your parking spot. Incidentally, the chef has done quite a good job at parking us here, against this white background.

3.
That parking ticket was justified, though! I saw it when I was lying in a crate in the back of the car, waiting to be fried. That officer was so surprised to see us lying there!

8.
Yeah, man! I really feel that we are lying together here, nice and cosy. Well-parked, indeed! I'm only curious to see who will be eating us. I hope it won't be that parking officer.

5.

Yes, but that's because he didn't get that ticket until he returned to his car on the parking lot in front of the butcher's!

1.

If you eat me with some meat, you will taste a nice peppery flavour! By the way, I was picked in person by the Creative Chef this morning.

4.

When the chef took me away from the butcher's, I didn't even notice that he was mad.

2.

But you shouldn't forget about me! I am made out of angry tomatoes; smashed against the wall, because the chef was angry due to a parking ticket!

All right,

a bit of a story about marketing and what it does to our perception of what food is, what is tasty and what doesn't taste good. I'll tell you a short story, which I hope will be of use to you.

Imagine the following. You eat a peach, but the peach is not ripe yet. Most people will experience it as a sour, hard and unpleasant fruit. You probably will too, which will lead you to throwing away the fruit.

Now imagine that you and I are about to found a new company. A company that trades peaches. Not just peaches, but delicious hard, sour and unripe peaches. Peaches that taste delicious with savoury dishes. For instance with a tomato salad.

My proposal is to call the unripe peach the TOMATO PEACH. We ensure that the peach is positioned next to the tomatoes in the vegetable department and not next to the ripe peaches in the fruit department. Oh, yes, and we give this new vegetable product an exclusive air by making it nice and expensive.

Then we make sure that several recipes with unripe peaches pop up on blogs across the internet. We will ask newspapers to write about it and with any luck it will

take off and become a success. After two years, the two of us will be chilling in the Bahamas because we have sold our 'unripe peaches' company. In the meantime, many other peach farmers have brought a similar product on the market. Naturally, they thought to themselves: "Those guys need much less time to harvest; let's do that too!"

All right, and what is the result? Over a period of 5 to 10 years, you'll see that the taste experience of a peach will have changed for

many people to being a sourer and harder product.
People will no longer feel the need to spit out unripe peaches when they eat one.

And then?

Yes, the two of us will hit them hard with a new company! SWEET PEACHES.

Extremely expensive, juicy peaches. Peaches sooooo sweet that they make you happier. Moreover, they are full of antioxidants and if you eat five per day, you even lose weight. By the way, did you know that all the movie stars in Hollywood eat this peach? As it turns out, it makes you slightly younger, it's great against baldness and people that eat peaches will on average live 2 years longer than people that eat unripe peaches.

SAVOURY PEACH SALAD

SALAD

> 2 unripe peaches
> 1/2 cucumber
> 4 sweet tomatoes
> 1 shallot
> Lemon juice
> Pepper and salt

Chop all ingredients into small cubes and mix with the lemon juice. Sprinkle some pepper and salt over it.

DRESSING

> 1 unripe peach
> 1 tsp. mustard
> 1 tsp. vinegar
> 4 tbsp. olive oil

Add the unripe peach to the juicer and collect the juice. Mix the juice with the vinegar and the mustard and slowly mix in the oil.

SERVE

Before serving the salad, read the story on this page to your guests. You will notice that it will yield much food for conversation.

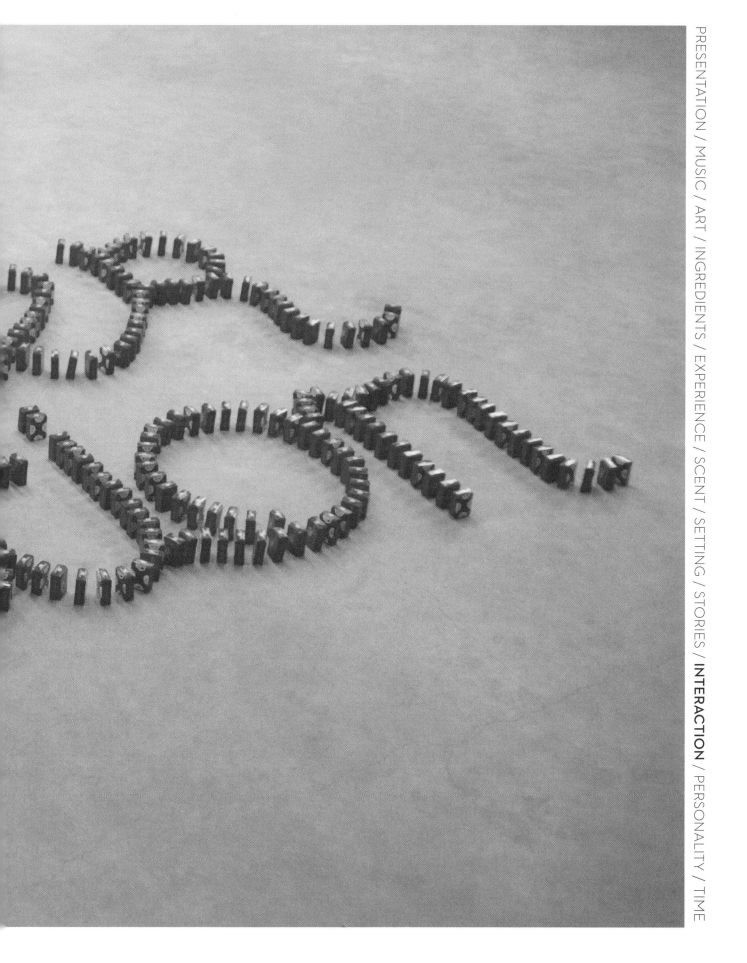

Interaction can easily be influenced by what the chef cooks. But also the table decoration can add to this. What can really contribute to increasing the interactive character of your dinner, is introducing a game element.

Let the games begin!

The Cook-Off

For whomever would like to spice up their daily cooking ritual, I've come up with The Cook-Off! Test your skills, pace, creativity, agility and improvisation skills in the kitchen. It is based on the BBC programme 'Ready Steady Cook'. But then at your own home.

GROCERY SHOPPING

Let your roommate/children/ partner/friends do grocery shopping for an amount agreed upon in advance. The idea is that they do shopping in a playful and strategic manner, to make it extra tough on the chef.

The party shopping for groceries needs to make it hard on the chef, but not impossible, for instance by buying 1 kilo salt from the budget. After all, whoever does the shopping has to eat the end result!

READY STEADY GO!

The moment the grocery bag makes its way onto the table, the dinner guests call out together: "Let's Cook". You, as the chef, will then have to get started with the ingredients from the bag and the leftovers from the fridge to make a complete three-course meal within 20 minutes (advanced), 30 minutes (a bit more realistic) or 40 minutes (for the wimps).

All bought ingredients must be used!

ASSESSMENT

At the end of the dinner, the guests put a grade in a hat and the average grade is the result for that day. This competition can last a year and at the end of the year the person with the highest final grade wins the honorary title Super Chef. The certificate that goes with this title can be downloaded in PDF format from the website (www.creativechef.nl)

The judging needs to take into account to what extent the chef actually cooked something themselves and whether they did anything original with the ready-made products.

CHEAT SHEET FOR THE CHEF

> *Hide ice cubes with broth in the freezer.*
> *When the grocery shoppers are gone, you can sneakily get started with some chopping of the ingredients still left in your refrigerator.*
> *Prepare the food processors and pans in advance.*
> *Before the grocery shoppers return, switch on the kettle to boil some water.*
> *Do not do any dishes in between; that takes too much time!*
> *Try and think in broader terms!*
> *Pasta also tastes good when mixed with rice and quinoa!*
> *Sandwiches can be turned into a pizza sandwich!*
> *Broccoli can be used to make broccoli couscous.*
> *Use a bit of the vanilla ice cream left over from dessert in the dressing as a replacement for sugar.*
> *No vinegar? Boil some wine down!*
> *No oil or butter? Use the oil from tinned feta or sundried tomatoes.*
> *Some vegetables can be hollowed out and used as a deep plate. Which means you will still have used the ingredient!*
> *Serve ingredients as a snack with the drinks if you really don't know what to do with them.*
> *To broaden your thinking and creativity in the kitchen: Lettuce can be turned into lettuce soup with a juicer!*
> *Some vegetables can be served in your dessert! For example: tomatoes can be made into very sweet tomato jam and fennel can be cooked in a 1:1 ratio of liquid and sugar.*
> *Need a piping bag? Use the corner of a sandwich bag.*

MINIMAL NECESSITIES

> One knife
> One peeler
> One cutting board
> Two spoons
> Hand blender
> Oven (you can also cook things in the oven!)

CREATIVE CHEF CHALLENGES YOU!

Now that the previous pages have taught you various skills and details, you might perhaps also be ready for a bigger challenge. A Cook-Off for about 200 people?

Invite 200 people and have them bring one product from their own region. Your challenge is to turn all those ingredients into a true feast within 4 hours.

Once you commence the big Cook-Off, start off with all the most time-consuming tasks. So start with as much chopping, roasting in the oven, cooking, washing and marinating as possible. What usually happens with me is that the chopping and the washing slowly makes it clear which ingredients need to go with which dishes!

Furthermore, you will notice that impossible ingredients such as liquor work well with desserts, that your plan will always change, that limitations often lead to really innovative inventions and that you will mainly have to work incredibly fast! Your assistant chefs – yes, you will be needing some! – will have to work independently and communicate clearly. If at any point you are at a loss yourself, just say: "You think of your own solution for now."

At the start, the guests can place the products they brought on the table at the correct region on the map of your country or area.

And what to do with a surplus of ingredients?
Be creative with large numbers that are hard to work with. For example, for ingredients such as cherries, simply create The Big Cherry Pit Spitting Game. Or use an excess of apples for apple bingo. Guaranteed success!

┌─ **TIPS** ─┐
› *Make sure you drink enough water.*
› *Stand up straight; that is better for your back.*
› *Think in combinations, not in what something will look like eventually. Presentation is not of any concern until the end and it just blocks you in thinking of possibilities.*
› *Don't take on this kind of challenge if you don't enjoy it.*
› *Place some beers in the fridge at the start, so you can enjoy them when the work is done!*

└─ **SUCCESS!** ─┘

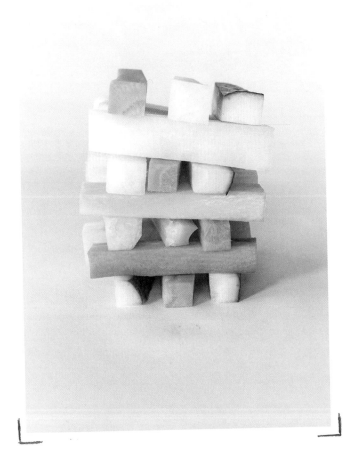

THE SNACK GAMES

Serve each game with delicious dip of finely chopped chives, yoghurt and pepper.

JENGA CRUDITE

Remove some vegetable sticks without knocking over the tower! *Thanks to Creative Chef Eva Strolenberg!*

MIKADO CRUDITE

Fun to place on standing tables at a mixer or to serve instead of bread at dinners where people don't know each other!

You are allowed to eat when you strike one of your opponent's pieces

CHESS AND CHECKERS WITH SNACKS

Chessboards and checkerboards are perfect for arranging snacks on. *Note: you only get to eat a snack when you strike one of your opponent's pieces!*

MARBLES

A plate that turns into a marble hole upon flipping over! Fun to do and you can use the marble hole for the sauce. *Design by Creative Chef Warni van Mierlo.*

Don't forget to bring your flower guide, as you might find something that you can add to the salad!

No picnic basket? Just use an old suitcase!

Picnicking with real plates and normal glassware is much more fun than using disposable material!

Picnic games:
Jeux de boules with fruit
Pinecone throwing
Discus throwing with plates
Paintball with fresh eggs
Marble play board

PICNIC

It is certainly a food experience! Picnicking might just be the most fun way to casually create a nice food experience without all too much hassle.

What does 'picnic' actually mean? It comes from the French term 'pique nique' and means something like 'picking out something small'.

The Creative Chef therefore suspects that it has more to do with picking out small dishes and bites, rather than picking a spot in nature to sit on a blanket.

Leave at home:
- Your telephone
- Many sweet dishes! They attract insects and can truly turn your picnic into an annoying occasion.

If you really want to go sustainable, you can take a solar cooker with you to heat up the frankfurters.

This cooker runs on solar power, enabling you to cook outdoors.

Did you know that a cooler is often called a Frigobox in Belgium?

It's also fun to know something about the background of the place where you will go picnicking. You can then tell your fellow picnickers about it.

Wish to truly make something exciting of this trip? Then hide a treasure and make a treasure map for your guests!

Bad weather?
Then simply picnic inside!

Scent
You'll smell enough grass!
Sound
Bird sounds work well for an indoor picnic.
Fun
You can also play croquet indoors!
Are you mad?
Project a beautiful outside landscape on the wall with a projector!
Have you lost your mind!?!
If you are really on a roll, simply place some trees inside and hang bottles of apple juice on them and place some presents under them for your guests.

INDOOR PICNIC

FRESH PIZZAS

Bake the pizza bases in advance. Those can then be covered with fresh ingredients such as salad, dried sausage, cheese and roasted vegetables.

SKEWERS

Skewers with tasty ingredients such as sausage, gherkins, tomatoes, slices of baguette, cubes of cheese and olives.

TREASURE CHEST

Make a grab box with vegetable crisps in it and a golden ticket. With the golden ticket you win immunity from washing the dishes when you get home!

WRAPS

Make wraps with e.g. chicken, salad and cream cheese. You can easily eat these from your hand without spilling and you can easily prepare them well in advance.

LUXURY

Blinis with salmon (see the page on the Tsar dinner) or oysters also work well for an indoor picnic.

JUICES

Serve a nice juice instead of soda.

(INTER)ACTION DURING THE DINNER

Interaction? What could be such a dinner during which it would be nice if people truly get to chat with each other and some dynamism emerges? Exactly, a wedding dinner during which the families can take the time to get a bit better acquainted. So during this dinner, we will have groups of guests alternatively working on tasks!

1 Try to keep the groups a bit varied or choose to divide them according to a common denominator: all men, grandfathers and grandmothers, or children.

2 Avoid complicated dishes with lengthy preparation times. Should you wish to have a stew that needs 4 hours to simmer anyway, then take care of it yourself.

3 In order to manage the process well, create an instruction and recipe for each course.

4 Always name one person per group who has the role of lead chef. This person also has the task to present the dish to the guests at the table.

5 Make it into a competition. Which group cooked the fastest, created the most beautiful plate and what presentation was the most fun? Most importantly: which dish tasted the best?

6 The group that wins, earns a dinner cooked by the bridal couple!

Each course needs to be arranged on the plate and served by another group. Ensure a good mix of people who know each other and people who don't know each other.

This is the perfect way to interrupt the dinner and talk with people who are not your table companions. It is also more intimate, as you will not need any waiters, only a good (creative) chef!

New York-style Burger

VEGETARIAN HAMBURGER

The hamburger made for the guests of the bridal couple in this case was a very delicious and healthy one. The couple lives in New York (hence the hamburger) and consider healthy food very important.

VEGGIE BURGER (12 PIECES)

> 800 grams chickpeas
> 100 grams seaweed
> 100 grams nuts
> 500 grams potato, boiled and peeled
> 150 grams egg
> 3 tablespoon soy
> 3 tablespoons ketchup
> 1 tablespoon porcini powder

Blend all ingredients in the food processor/blender and make them into hamburgers. If the burgers are too sticky, sprinkle them with some flour. Take your time to fry them in a frying pan and gather them on a baking tray. Keep the burgers warm in the oven at 60 degrees.

SERVE

> 12 brioche buns
> Edible flowers
> Seaweed salad
> Lettuce
> Yellow carrot, cut into fries
> Mayonnaise

Place the bun on the plate. Put the lettuce, some seaweed salad, mayonnaise and a burger on top. Add the second bun, secure with a skewer and decorate with the flowers. Serve with the yellow carrot fries - if that is too healthy for you, then simply make real fries.

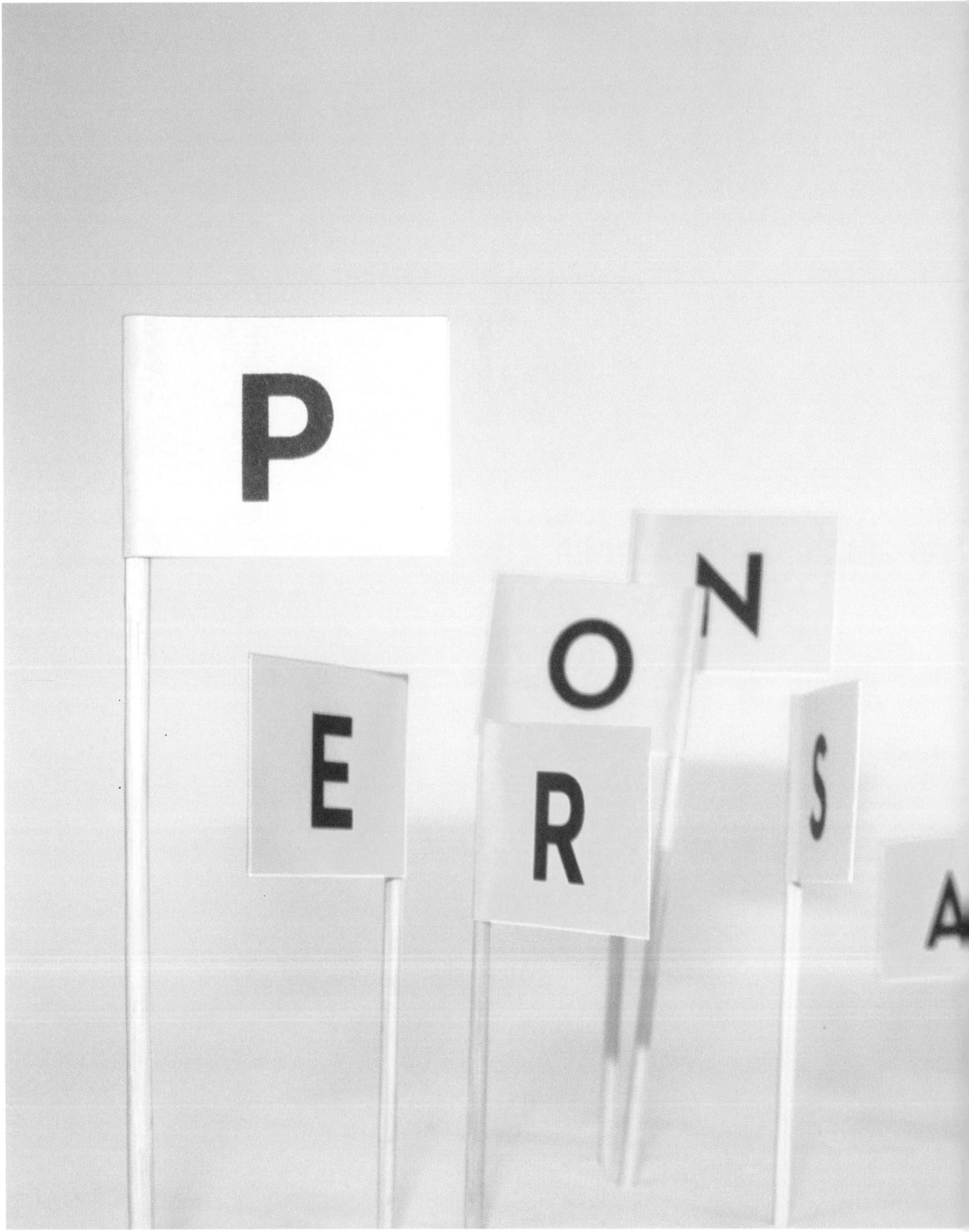
P
O
N
E
R
S

The most beautiful achievement for a chef is to get as close as possible to the soul of each person he or she cooks for. In other words, can you take the childhood memories, first tastes, and the character of this person and translate it into their ultimate dinner. That's not easy, but you can go a long way!

THE ULTIMATE DINNER FOR TWO

'How To Go About Doing That' Handbook

OK, say you wish to do something really special for a couple that you know. They did something extraordinary for you and now you want to give them something personal... Well, here's what you need to do.

Organise the ultimate dinner for 2

> Set a date.
> Arrange for someone to pick them up from home and bring them back again in the evening.
> Arrange a beautiful, special location that has cooking facilities.

Have them complete the following questionnaire

1. PICK ONE OF THE FOLLOWING CHARACTER TRAITS THAT FITS YOU MOST:

gentle   dreamy   strict   sloppy
            free spirit   conservative   sweet   tidy
quiet   high energy   ambitious   domestic
        frequent traveller   emotional   rational

2. OUR FAVOURITE HOLIDAY DESTINATION IS ....

3. IF WE HAD TO CHOOSE BETWEEN FISH, MEAT OR CHEESE ....
....

4. IF I COMPARED MY PARTNER WITH A FISH IN THE SEA, IT WOULD HAVE TO BE
....

5. OUR FAVOURITE PASTA SAUCE IS ....

6. WHEN I THINK OF MY CHILDHOOD, MY FAVOURITE DISH FROM MY GRANDMOTHER IS ....

7. FIRM OR SOFT? ....

8. OUR FAVOURITE SCENTS ARE ....

1. CHARACTER TRAITS

This information will allow you to create the perfect welcome cocktail. Make a drink from Moscato d'Asti and complete it with the ingredients that match the character traits of the couple.

Gentle
Peach coulis
Dreamy
Apricot coulis
Strict
Vodka
Sloppy
Fruit beer
Free spirit
Hemp juice
Frequent traveller
Piña colada
Emotional
White chocolate ice cream
Rational
Nothing
Conservative
Champagne
Sweet
Strawberry coulis
Tidy
Lemon juice
Quiet
Green tea
High energy
Red Bull
Ambitious
Absinth (if that is too ambitious: Pernod)
Domestic
Boerenjongens (Dutch dish of raisins soaked in brandy)

2. OUR FAVOURITE HOLIDAY DESTINATION

> *South of France*

Place your guests across from each other without a table, as you will be serving the table with a map on it!

> Small bottles of wine from the region
> Shrimps in the sea
> Brandade de Moreau uit Toulon
> Bouillabaisse from the port of Marseille
> Sausage from the Provence
> Nougat from Montéllimar
> Pâté from Lyon
> Goat cheese from Corsica
> Aioli and olive tapenade from Nice
> Duck confit from Carcassonne
> Ham from Bayonne
> Aubergine caviar from Niort

3. IF WE HAD TO CHOOSE BETWEEN FISH, MEAT OR CHEESE

> *Cheese*

The first course is a hit from our kitchen, which you can easily vary with the main ingredient. Should your guest answer with 'meat', then you can use small pieces of jamón ibérico. If their answer is 'fish', then small marinated squids go well with this dish. Our guests opted for cheese, so we chose to add Burrata Pugliese.

Salad of various tomato varieties with Burrata Pugliese.

> Tomato caviar
> Tiger tomato
> Haut Clos tomato
> Melon in balls
> Unripe peach
> Cucumber
> Basil flowers
> Truffle potato crisps
> Burrata Pugliese
> Balsamico di Modena

Chop all the ingredients. Scoop four little balls from the melon with a melon baller. Take four nice long strips from the cucumber. Cut the tomatoes in quarters and the peach in thin slices. Place everything in a deep plate and top it off with a spoon of tomato caviar. Cover with the burrata and decorate the dish with some truffle potato crisps and basil flowers. Finish with the balsamic vinegar.

SERVING SUGGESTION
Scent
Creative Chef's perfume No. 1
Music
Italian music

4. IF I COMPARED MY PARTNER WITH A FISH IN THE SEA, IT WOULD HAVE TO BE...

> *She is a langoustine. He a salmon.*

Place a photo frame around your iPad. That way you can playfully use it as a plate.

RECIPE

> **4 langoustines**
> **Wild salmon, suitable for sashimi**
> **Seaweed**
> **Indian cress leaves**
> **Oyster leaves**
> **Wasabi**
> **Soy sauce**

VIDEO SUGGESTIONS

Fun videos that you can play with this fish duo are:
> *All episodes of Earth that cover the sea*
> *Anything by Jacques Cousteau*
> *Finding Nemo*
> *Demonstration videos for sport fishing*
> *Episodes of 'Deadliest Catch' from the Discovery channel*
> *Video of your goldfish*

5. OUR FAVOURITE PASTA SAUCE

> *Pesto*

All right, this is a winner. Do you know the scene from the Disney film *Lady and the Tramp?*

RECIPE FOR EXTREMELY LONG SPAGHETTI

> **1 egg**
> **100 grams of flour for pasta dough**
> **Teaspoon of olive oil**

Make a hole in the flour and pour the egg and the oil into it. Knead until you get a smooth and shiny dough. Run through a pasta machine, starting at the thickest setting and repeating until you have reached setting 8. Cut long strands of spaghetti from the dough. Cook until the pasta starts floating.
Carefully run the pasta through your guests' favourite sauce.

SERVING TIP

Take a picture of the kissing moment and send it to them after the dinner via text message, thanking them for their presence. Perhaps next time they'll invite you and your partner for an ultimate dinner for two!

6. WHEN I THINK OF MY CHILDHOOD, MY FAVOURITE DISH FROM MY GRANDMOTHER IS...

> ## *Indonesian rice table*

Everyone has their own memories from the past and the food they used to love at grandma's house!
A recipe for a mini rice table:

CREATIVE CHEF'S RENDANG

> **400 grams of beef cheek without membranes**
  Distribute the beef cheek across two portions and fry in some oil in the saucepan.
> **Salt and pepper**
  Add some salt and pepper. Not too much!
> **2 sweet and large onions**
  Chop into cubes and add to the pan.
> **2 cloves of garlic**
  Chop roughly and add.
> **20 grams of fresh ginger**
  Add the chopped ginger.
> **Small red pepper without seeds**
  Chop the pepper really fine and add to the pan.
> **500 grams of beef stock**
  Add.
> **300 grams of tomato puree**
  Add.
> **5 tablespoons of ketjap manis sauce**
  Also add.

Let the whole mixture simmer as softly as possible for about 8 hours. You can also place the pan in the oven at 120 degrees throughout the night; that will make the meat truly tender!

ACAR

> **Half a cucumber**
  Cut into slices.
> **Half a red bell pepper**
  Cut into strips.
> **A bit of white cabbage**
  Also cut into strips.
  Bring the water to a boil
  Submerse the vegetables in the boiling water for two minutes.
> **1 clove of garlic and 1 cm fresh ginger**
> **1 tsp. turmeric**
> **125 ml white wine vinegar**
> **2 tbsp. sugar**

Mix these ingredients in a food processor and let vegetables soak in this for a night.

MINI QUAIL EGG WITH CURRY SAUCE

> **4 small quail eggs, boiled and peeled**
  Briefly fry these in some hot oil.
> **1 dl coconut milk**
  Add to the mix.
> **1 tsp. trassi (Asian supermarket)**
> **1 tsp. lemongrass powder**
> **1 tsp. turmeric**
> **2 cloves of garlic**

Add them all. As soon as the sauce is bound, you can serve the dish.

SERVING TIP

> *Naturally, you serve it with rice!*
> *Also serve with a mini-skewer: cocktail stick with chicken and peanut sauce.*
> *Serve the rice table on a banana leaf. Before serving the rice table, roast some spices such as cinnamon and cloves. This way, you ensure a pleasant Indonesian aroma.*

7. FIRM OR SOFT?

> *Soft*

COURSE NUMBER SEVEN IS THE CHEESE PLATTER!

When you get the answer 'soft' you serve

> **St Maure cheese**
> **Brillat savarin**
> **Epoisse cheese**
> **Gorgonzola**

When you get the answer 'firm' you serve

> **Tomme de savoie**

Leave the cheeses on a warm spot and put a glass bell over them. That way the smell will be enormous and very overwhelming. You could check page number 138 what cheeses to use to make it into a cacophony of smelliness!

8. OUR FAVOURITE SCENTS

> *Peach and strawberry*

The final course is based on a dish with white chocolate cream with fresh fruit and delicious scents from scented candles.

RECIPE

> White peach
> Strawberry
> Ginger snaps
> 100 grams Greek yoghurt
> Honey, to taste
> 100 grams white chocolate

Cut the fruit in discs. In the meantime, melt the chocolate au bain marie (or in simple English: in a bowl above hot water) and stir until the white chocolate has melted. Stir a little bit through the yoghurt so that the substances can get used to each other. Then stir the yoghurt into the chocolate and cover with plastic foil. Let it harden in the fridge until use. Place a small dot of chocolate cream on each plate. Stick a ginger snap to it. Add the rest of the chocolate cream on top of the ginger snap with the use of a piping bag. Place pieces of fruit on it. Add another ginger snap on top.

SCENTED CANDLES

You can buy them, but you could also make them yourself! The greatest tip is to make an olive oil candle with essential oils.

WHAT TO DO?

Mix some drops of essential oil with some olive oil. Add a candlewick and light it.

SERVING TIP

Sit near it with a nice dessert wine or a cup of coffee. You guests will certainly appreciate it if you come sit with them at this point. In doing so you give them the chance to thank you!

Allright, now it's your turn!

YOU ARE WHAT YOU EAT

Ask a random person what he or she enjoys eating most, and you already have a wealth of knowledge about that person. I find it fascinating to hear my guests' stories about food. If you ask an Italian, he or she will almost always name an Italian dish, including the maker of the dish. If you ask a Dutch or American person, you will usually hear more international dishes.

Daan from the Netherlands is on a quick break from his food truck, where he serves delicious meat dishes. And if he could choose for himself, he would opt for his mother's pilaf.

Audar, Sultan and Sanira from Kyrgyzstan like horsemeat
a lot. Especially in a stew with potato, onion and flour.

Werner from Linz, Austria, was raised on the Wiener Schnitzel. It remains
his favourite dish, but only the real one with veal.

Mohammed from Abu Dabi (capital of the United Arabic
Emirates) mainly thinks sweet dishes are the bomb! His
favourite food is therefore cake and pie!

Andor is from Poland and lives in Warsaw. He loves
typical Polish dishes, but his favourite is... pizza.

Fufu soup is the bite that this boss loves most! He doesn't
want to tell us his name. Fufu soup is a popular dish with yams.
It is a delightfully sweet and savoury dish that is eaten in many
countries in Africa!

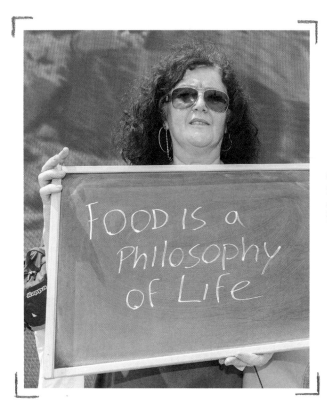

Giovanna is a chef at Antica Osteria in Cormons, Italy. The town is located east of Venice. This woman lives for, from and through food.

This barman from Poland is called Rafal and he collects signatures. He loves hard work, beer and the pierogi of his mother. Pierogis are a type of dumplings with a savoury filling. Rafal likes them best with sauerkraut.

The Doliny family from Miami, USA, cannot reach any consensus! Pancakes with Nutella for mum. Dad is sticking to cheeseburgers. The daughters prefer omelette and sushi and the smallest can't decide!

Shiva from Teheran, Iran, is as modest as she writes! If you look closely, you can see that she wrote the name of a traditional Iranian dish with rice, nuts and pomegranate.

Time and food. You can use time in various manners to create the ultimate food experience. By making use of the time you can put your patience to the test; the taste of meat cooked for 24 hours is better than the taste of meat cooked for 6 hours. And not just because of the 24 hours it has been simmering, but also because it is in the back of your mind!

Time also brings the perspective of other ages. How did people eat in the past?

Take your time and enjoy your eating experience.

PIZZA VEGETARIANA

Slow Food Style Ingredients :
> Patience
> Passion
> A vegetable garden
or a greenhouse

PLANT SEEDS

First off, we will be planting the following seeds:

> Tomato plant
> Onion seed
> Bell pepper seed
> Courgette seed
> Rucola seed
> Basil seed
> Wheat

BUILDING A WOOD-FIRED OVEN

Then we build our own wood-fired oven fire. Because let's be honest: pizzas from a wood-fired oven are the best, aren't they?!

Apply for a licence and hope for the best. If this doesn't work out, order a mobile wood-fired oven from the internet. Then you can even bring it along on holidays! Subsequently, check out some sites on the internet for tips on building an oven and get started. You can even pick out your own construction kit.

HARVEST

As soon as the wheat is ripe, we can start to harvest. Separate the wheat from the chaff and mill the wheat into flour.
Perhaps you can best have this done by a professional miller.

MAKING MOZZARELLA

> 4 litres of fresh whole milk
> 2 tsp. citric acid
> 1/4 tsp. rennet

Bring 4 litres of milk to a boil up to 32 degrees in an acid-resistant pan (thus no aluminium). Add the citric acid. Then add the rennet and stir for 5 minutes. Take off the fire and leave on for 20 minutes.
If all goes well, the milk will curdle. Cut the curdled milk with a knife in small cubes of 1 cm. Dress a sieve with a cheesecloth and let the cubes of curdled milk drain out in it until it no longer drip. Place the remaining mass for one minute in the microwave at full capacity. Knead nice balls of cheese from it. Don't forget to use rubber gloves! Add some salt to the drainage liquid and use it to store the cheese in for a week!

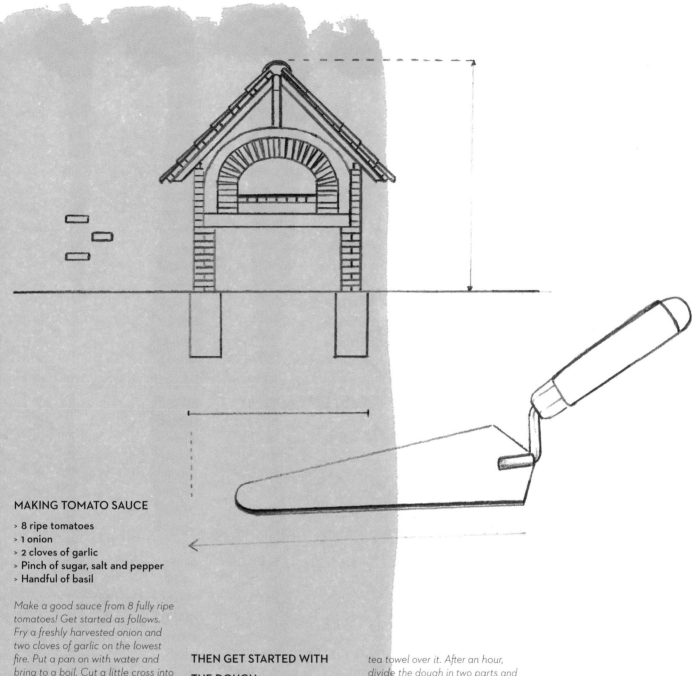

MAKING TOMATO SAUCE

> 8 ripe tomatoes
> 1 onion
> 2 cloves of garlic
> Pinch of sugar, salt and pepper
> Handful of basil

Make a good sauce from 8 fully ripe tomatoes! Get started as follows. Fry a freshly harvested onion and two cloves of garlic on the lowest fire. Put a pan on with water and bring to a boil. Cut a little cross into each tomato and immerse them in the hot water for 10 seconds. Then briefly immerse them in iced water and peel the skins off. Chop into cubes and add to the onions without the seeds. Add a pinch of sugar, salt and pepper. Leave to simmer for a bit. After thirty minutes, add freshly cut basil and take off the fire. Let the sauce mature in taste by storing it in the refrigerator for two days.
Heat up the oven with self-cut wood two hours in advance! Then harvest the fresh vegetables that will later on end up on the pizza.

THEN GET STARTED WITH THE DOUGH

> 1/2 bag of dried yeast
> 1 tsp. sugar
> 250 grams self-made flour
> 2 tbsp. olive oil
> 1/2 tsp. salt

Dissolve the yeast in some hand-warm water with sugar. Place a little heap of the flour on the worktop and make a hole in which you can place the yeast mixture. Stir through the dough and add salt, oil and two tablespoons of water. Knead the entire mix and leave it to rise in a warm place with a moist

tea towel over it. After an hour, divide the dough in two parts and make two beautiful razor-thin pizza bases. Spread these with tomato sauce. Chop thin onion rings, slices of courgette, strips of bell peppers and mushroom and add to the pizza. Then cut the cheese into cubes and sprinkle the pizza with this. Finish off with fresh basil and some pepper and salt. Bake to finish in the wood-fired oven and pick some fresh rucola. Add the rucola together with some oil to the pizza and – after slaving away for a year – take a seat to truly enjoy this pizza! You have a right to be proud of the end result, right?

FAST, FAST, FAST

Fast? Fast food is not that fast at all! A carrot or an apple is ready to eat much quicker than a hamburger. Fruit is thus actually the most ideal ready-made fast food there is!

The perfect way to relax is to take your time and bake a delightful apple pie! Below you'll find the perfect relaxation recipe.

Go out for some groceries and have a nice cup of coffee with a friend you run into and haven't spoken to in a long time. After 2 hours of catching up, decide that it is time to get together sometime and cook for each other. Take a moment to consider and decide to invite your friend the very same day to bake an apple pie together. Settle the bill and head to the shop where you will be able to get all the ingredients.

> **300 grams of self-rising flour**
> **200 grams of cold butter**
> **160 grams of brown sugar**
> **1 bag of vanilla sugar**
> **1 beaten egg**
> **Pinch of salt**

FOR THE FILLING:

> **1 kg hard, sour apples (Bell de Boskoop or Jonagold)**
> **1 tbsp. lemon juice**
> **15 grams of sugar**
> **2 tsp. cinnamon**
> **60 grams of raisins**

1

Take your time and work with concentration as you cut the butter through the flour, brown sugar, vanilla sugar and salt using 2 knives. Massage the mixture with the butter until a crumbly mixture emerges. Add 3/4 of the egg. Wrap the dough in some foil and place it in the refrigerator.

2

Make a cup of tea and sit down for a bit. Get up and continue with the filling of the pie. Tip: why not put on some relaxing music, too?

3

Make the base from 2/5 of the dough. The circle for the base can also be cut into two and placed inside; that makes the process a little easier.

Roll out the rest of the dough as well, coat the inner sides and save some for the top.

5

Let it cool off for 5 minutes and trace the ridge with the knife to remove edge. Then place it in the fridge and let it cool off further.

4

Add the apple filling. Make strips and place them horizontally and vertically on the top. Coat the dough strips with the remaining egg. Set the oven at 175 degrees and bake the cake for 78 minutes.

WILD BOARS, FIRES, DOGMATIX AND JUGS WITH DRINK

That was the dinner I would dream of as a young boy: the dinner at the end of the comic Asterix and Obelix. With Bard, the minstrel who could not sing, wild boars, fires, Dogmatix and jugs with drink. But how did such things truly go in those days?

The Greek author Posidonius was able to observe how the Gauls actually lived back in the days of Asterix and Obelix.

When the Gauls dined, they sat on the ground on skins of wolves and dogs, in a circle at long wooden tables. He then describes the table setting and the serving, which was taken care of by young children. He continues: "Close to the place where they eat, there are fires burning with cauldrons and spits above them with meat."

It was Posidonius who noticed that the Gauls enjoyed:

roasting meat, eating fried fish with vinegar, as well as cumin. The Romans ate olive oil, so they refused to eat that. Wine, however, they considered divinely delicious. Furthermore, they drank wheat beer with a bit of honey. And they drank water with which they cleaned their honeycombs. They would drink from earthenware mugs. The food was served on earthenware plates. They did not use any cutlery, only knives to cut the meat. Not only did they eat wild boar, but also beef and mutton. Moreover, they ate lots of bread.

MAGIC POTION

Naturally, the dinner will not be a success without the magic potion. Below you'll find a list of ingredients that are in the potion, plus the ingredients we recommend that you use, should you wish to keep it drinkable for your guests!

THE PANORAMIX VERSION

> Strawberries
> Wild boar
> Fresh grass and wild flowers
> Four-leaf clovers
> Big omelette with cheese
> 1 gram duck with mandarins
> Handful of nuts
> One bird's foot
> Cloves of garlic
> Bay leaves
> 75 ml low-fat milk
> 4 drops of snake venom
> A few tea leaves
> 50 grams of fresh fish
> Spinach
> Bottle of liquid salamander
> 500 ml carrot juice
> 1 branch of mistletoe
> 5 litres water
> Add vegetables to taste
> Pinch of salt

CREATIVE CHEF'S VERSION

> Sweet tomatoes
> Wild boar or pig's leg
> Cornflower
> Vermicelli
> Tablespoon of duck fat
> Handful of hazelnuts
> Chicken carcass
> Garlic
> Bay leaves
> White wine
> 4 drops of Tabasco
> Tea leaves
> Anchovy fillets
> Spinach
> Salamander brandy
  (Check: this drink actually exists in Slovenia)
> Carrot juice
> Branch of mistletoe
> Water
> Vegetables
> Pinch of salt

Of course, we won't reveal the real recipe. Throw everything together according to your own instinct and hope for the best. If this does not work out, ensure that the potion is at least tasty! Panoramix used a golden crescent to chop his products!

The little barrels complete the picture. Super fun fact: it took Luc hours to get them here and return them again.

Pork from the roasting spit

A Roman pillar works , too! These are often for sale at garden stores from the kitsch department.

GALLIC RECIPE

Roasted piglet from the spit with a salad of roasted beetroot, carrots and Leyden cheese.

THE PIG

Roasting a pig is no mean feat. It requires precision, patience and planning. Hereby a number of guidelines and necessities.

> A spit that is suitable for roasting a pig.
> Get a good pig that has had a good life (for instance from Lindenhoff in Baambrugge, the Netherlands). That tastes better and is well worth the preparation time.
> Always use wood or charcoal and avoid lighter cubes, lighter fluid and turpentine.
> A piglet or pig of 15 kg is enough for 30 people.
> Roasting a pig of 15 kg takes at least 4 hours.
> The secret to roasting a pig is indirect heat. Therefore, lay down 2 fires parallel to the roast (so not directly under the roast). Rub salt or dry rub into the roast.

(Dishes by Baaf and Roel of Varkensroosteren.nl)

SALAD OF ROASTED BEETROOT, CARROT AND LEYDEN CHEESE

This salad offers a beautiful play of full, sweet tastes and sours accompanied by a nutty flavour. The ideal accompaniment with a juicy piece of roasted pork from the spit. The recipe is for 30 people.

INGREDIENTS

> 1500 grams beetroot
> 1500 grams rainbow carrots
> olive oil
> 150 grams rucola
> 500 grams Leyden cheese
> White and red wine vinegar for sprinkling over the vegetables.

FOR THE DRESSING

> 37.5 ml red wine vinegar
> 37.5 ml white wine vinegar
> 75 gr. apple syrup

Leave the beetroot and the carrots whole. Preferably roast them in ashes. Do this by placing them at the outside edge of the fire on a layer of ashes. Then cover them with a good layer of warm ashes and glowing coals of approximately 10 to 15 cm. Avoid the red-hot coals. Ensure that this pile is located in the vicinity of the glowing charcoal fire. The radiation heat will ensure that the vegetables get cooked. After about 2 hours the vegetables will be done.

Then let the vegetables cool off. Peel the carrots and the beetroot. Cut the carrots in the length in four parts. Chop the carrots and beetroot in large chunks. First chop the carrots and then the beetroot, as the beetroot will give off a strong colour.

If necessary, the beetroot and the carrots can be roasted in the oven. Set the oven at 180 degrees Celsius and roast for 1 to 1.5 hours. Take them out of the oven as soon as they are al dente. The carrots will be done quicker than the beetroot.

Store the vegetables separately. Sprinkle the beetroot with red wine vinegar and the carrots with the white wine vinegar.

The ideal side dish

Make the dressing as follows: bring 75 ml water to a boil in a small saucepan. Dissolve the apple syrup in the water. Add taste to the dressing by adding pepper, salt and equal parts white and red wine vinegar.

Roughly grate the Leyden cheese. This works best by grating the cheese unevenly using a cheese grater. Shape the pieces in whatever way you see fit.

Mix part of the dressing into the vegetables. Then mix this with the rucola. Place the mix in the bowl. Subsequently, sprinkle with the grated cheese and the remainder of the dressing. Serve immediately.

The specific circumstance will influence the cooking and the duration of the preparation of various ingredients. The noted times offer a guideline. Let your experience and observations during the preparation lead you.

Use plates
of red clay or
simply eat with
your hands.

TO CONCLUDE

I hope you have enjoyed this book. Please don't hesitate to let our team know what you reeeaaally enjoyed, didn't like as much, or simply found ridiculous! We have worked on this for a long time and would like to work on similar projects in the future, so all feedback is welcome! I hereby thank you, the reader, for taking the time to read and leaf through this book. Now it's time to honour a number of special people and companies.

JASPER

In particular, I would like to thank my greatest treasure on earth: Annelien, my wife, biggest love and the person who has been supporting me and stimulating me all these years to do what I now get to do. Furthermore, you have given me the ultimate experience ever, Annelien, by giving me the gift of two children. Jent and Meesje. Jent and Meesje, if you are reading this a few years down the line (as soon as you are old enough): daddy loves you! Mum and Dad: never underestimate how great your influence has been on my life, in a positive sense! Mum, your cooking skills are the best. And dad, thank you for all your good advice and financial support when it was necessary! You two are the best. Moreover, the rest of the family also deserves my gratitude! Special mention for Sjoerd: you know it, we did it! Piet Heijn and Jan Joost: thanx boys, you have given me so much awesomeness all these years! And not to be forgotten, my fellow countrymen of Boubadioup, Jochem, Jeroen, Schelto and Tom: we make the world smile!!

Furthermore, I would like to thank my big sources of inspiration: Luc Janssens, Art Blakey, Michel Bras, Questlove, Frank Zappa, the Bouba Boys, Jackson Pollock and my dog, Truffel. My favourite dish? German Currywurst!!!

LUC JANSSENS

I'd like to thank Miran and my children Cas and Roos, because they give me tons of energy and motivation (and they always come and join me in the kitchen for some fun tasting). My mother, as she taught me how to cook when I was just a kid; my father, because he always believed in me. He would have loved this project. My brother, because he pushes me and for his alternative perspectives. My in-laws for their support and enthusiasm.
My sources of inspiration: First off Jazzy, because he is an unstoppable idea generator. Furthermore, Pierre Gagniere for his gastronomic genius and Michael Caines for his 'everything is possible' mentality. Ang Lee for his film 'Eat Drink Man Woman'. Jimi Hendrix, Isaac Hayes and Marvin Gaye for their fat soul.

ROGIER BOOGAARD

The pictures in my head were making their way to the paper. Jasper thank you for taking me with you on this creative and inspiring journey, it was a blast! I owe a lot to my lovely girlfriend, Karin. You stimulate me to fly around with my camera, always in search for places where my thoughts are looking for! I love you!
My photography started early on, when I wanted to look in the lens at a young age. Dad, you are not with us anymore, but your passion for photography made me what I am today! Mom, thanks for your support. Thanks to you I learned the values about good food, a great gift! I love you both. And of course my two sisters, Marieke and Jorine. We live nearby and I enjoy sharing 'those little moments of joy'.
Last but not least I give a shout out to all my friends. You make me feel rich and happy, and forgive me when I point my camera at you guys again. Sorry but I can't help it!

SUBSODA

We had a lot of fun mixing, chopping and cooking all of Jasper's creative concoctions into this cookbook. There were days when our studio seemed more like a kitchen than a graphic and illustrative design agency... We're looking forward to trying all the recipes!

PLUS The team of Creative Chefs that contributed to this super adventure!
Jessy Rietdijk and Hanne Ghijsen of subsoda
Rogier Boogaard
Saskia de Wal
Warni van Mierlo
Bas van Hattum
Malou van de Vegt
Timo Venhuis
Baaf en Roel van Varkensroosteren.nl
Eva Strolenberg
Reinier Suurenbroek
Wouter de Winter
Marjon Hogervorst
Irina Raiu
Elise Yuksl
Henk van Berkel and the BijenAkker
Suzan Becking
And of course the following heroes, without whom all of this would not exist: Food Jazz & DJs, de Koekfabriek, Voor de Kunst, de BijenAkker, Kookmeesters, KUUB, Dille en Kamille, Houtzagerij, Hanos ISPC Utrecht, Sissy Boy, Servir Frais, Boubadioup en de Paradidles, Domvorm Creative Studio, Lindenhoff, the Food Line Up, Foodinspiration, Willem en Drees.